Robert K. White, MA, CEAP
Deborah George Wright, MA
Editors

Addiction Intervention
Strategies to Motivate Treatment-Seeking Behavior

Pre-publication
REVIEWS,
COMMENTARIES,
EVALUATIONS . . .

"**M**any patients suffering from alcoholism and other addictions cannot reach out for help. Consequently, too many patients suffering from these diseases die if interventions are not expertly performed. *Addiction Intervention* provides clear, concise, and skillful guidance for such interventions, complemented by an excellent reference list for further reading. I would highly recommend this book to therapists, practitioners, and students."

G. Douglas Talbott, MD
President of the American Society
of Addiction Medicine,
Medical Director, Talbott Recovery
Campus; Atlanta, GA

"**A**mong the excellent books in the field, *Addiction Intervention* is paramount. The contributors offer a practical guide for both the entry-level participant and the experienced professional. This book is a must in anybody's library and will be of invaluable assistance in planning interventions."

Maxwell M Weisman, MD
Former Director,
Maryland State Alcoholism
Control Administration;
Faculty Member,
Johns Hopkins University
and the University of Maryland,
Baltimore, MD

The Haworth Press, Inc.

NOTES FOR PROFESSIONAL LIBRARIANS AND LIBRARY USERS

This is an original book title published by The Haworth Press, Inc. Unless otherwise noted in specific chapters with attribution, materials in this book have not been previously published elsewhere in any format or language.

CONSERVATION AND PRESERVATION NOTES

All books published by The Haworth Press, Inc. and its imprints are printed on certified pH neutral, acid free book grade paper. This paper meets the minimum requirements of American National Standard for Information Sciences–Permanence of Paper for Printed Material, ANSI Z39.48-1984.

Addiction Intervention
Strategies to Motivate Treatment-Seeking Behavior

HAWORTH Addictions Treatment
F. Bruce Carruth, PhD
Senior Editor

Addiction Intervention
Strategies to Motivate Treatment-Seeking Behavior

Robert K. White, MA, CEAP
Deborah George Wright, MA
Editors

The Haworth Press
New York • London

Cover design by Monica L. Seifert.

The Haworth Press, Inc., 10 Alice Street, Binghamton, NY 13904-1580

Library of Congress Cataloging-in-Publication Data

Addiction intervention : strategies to motivate treatment-seeking behavior / Robert K. White, Deborah George Wright, editors.
     p.   cm.
   Includes bibliographical references and index.
   ISBN 0-7890-0434-8 (alk. paper).
   1. Substance abuse—Patients—Rehabilitation. 2. Crisis intervention (Psychiatry) 3. Substance abuse—Treatment. 4. Psychiatric referral. I. White, Robert Kenneth, 1931- . II. Wright, Deborah George.
RC564.A283 1998
362.29′18—dc 21
                                               97-37000
                                                 CIP

To my father,
John D. White, Lt. Commander, U.S. Navy, retired,
whose sixteen years of sobriety following
a family intervention inspired this book;
Vernon Johnson, who developed the family intervention technique;
Bob Miller; and all of the health professionals
and family members who search for a way to help
the still-suffering alcoholic and drug dependent person.
We hope this book provides some direction.

Robert K. White

To my husband and interventionist, Robert Wright;
to his interventionist of eighteen years ago, Dr. Charles Snyder;
and to all the caring professionals who have the courage
to give people with chemical dependencies the hope,
the means, and the motivation to seek recovery—
you are my heroes.

Also to the memory of my father-in-law, Robert Wright Sr.,
his brother, Frank, and their father Frank Sr.,
and all those who lost their lives to alcohol or drug addiction
in a battle that they alone could not win.

Deborah George Wright

CONTENTS

ABOUT THE EDITORS

Robert K. White, MA, CEAP, is the Director of University Behavioral Health at the University of Maryland Medical System. His current responsibilities include managing employee assistance programs for the University of Maryland Medical System, the Baltimore Orioles major and minor league baseball teams, and the Baltimore Ravens NFL team, and he is a treatment professional for the NFL Drug Rehab Program. Mr. White holds a faculty appointment at the University of Maryland School of Medicine as Clinical Assistant Professor in the Department of Psychiatry; is a founding board member for the National Council on Alcoholism and Drug Dependence—Maryland Chapter; and is former Chairman of the Subcommittee on Drug-Free Workplace for the Governor's Executive Advisory Council in Maryland. He is a member of the National Association of Alcoholism & Drug Abuse Counselors, the Employees Professional Association, and the Certified Addiction Counselors of Maryland. He has presented numerous workshops on Intervention Strategies, Alcoholism and Drug Dependence Treatment, and Impaired Professionals for medical societies, hospital staff, medical students, and addiction professionals. His audiences have included the American Medical Association, the American Hospital Association, and the American Dental Association. He has published numerous articles in professional journals including *Journal of Community Psychology,* the *Maryland Medical Journal,* the *Journal of Addictive Diseases,* and the *Maryland State Dental Association Journal.*

Deborah G. Wright, MA, is Dean of Extended Learning at Southwestern Oregon Community College and cofounder of the Newmark Career and Opportunity Center—a model reemployment one-stop center that uses intervention in the integrated social services setting to develop skilled, drug-free workers for entry and mid-level positions. Ms. Wright has fifteen years of experience in the field of addiction intervention development. She cofounded and, for six years, served as a board member of a JCAH-accredited residential treatment program in Sun Valley, Idaho. She is the author of six intervention books, including *Creating and Maintaining the Drug-Free Workforce* (McGraw-Hill, 1993), *Dare to Confront* (Dell Books, 1991), *It's Your Business: Intervention for a Drug-Free Workplace* (Hazelden, 1991), and *Because You Care: Intervention Strategies in the Public Schools* (U.S. Department of Education, 1994). She has also written manuals for employee assistance and student assistance training programs. The former Director of the Institute for Drug and Alcohol Abuse Education, which won a national Drug-Free Schools award for a state-wide teacher training initiative, Ms. Wright was honored in 1994 with a State of Maryland Certificate of Achievement award for her work.

CONTRIBUTORS

James Crowley, MA, is a nationally recognized trainer, consultant, and facilitator with special expertise in student assistance programs, community collaboration, and alcohol, tobacco, and other drug-use intervention and prevention programs. For over fifteen years, he has traveled throughout the United States, presenting in a variety of conferences, seminars, and workshops.

Hon. Peggy F. Hora was elected to the Municipal Court of Alameda County (California) in 1984, and has served as that court's presiding judge, President of the California-Nevada Women Judges, on numerous planning committees, and as faculty for California Judicial Education and Research (CJER). She is currently Dean of the B. E. Witkin Judicial College of California. Judge Hora has taught on the subjects of alcohol and other drugs to the courts for both California and the National Judicial College, has presented at every national drug court conference, and has lectured in such diverse states as Utah, Minnesota, Hawaii, and Colorado. She has published a number of articles on substance abuse, with a particular emphasis on pregnant and parenting women.

David McDuff, MD, joined the full-time faculty at the University of Maryland in 1988 after spending ten years on active duty as a psychiatrist in the U.S. Army. He is currently the Director of the Department of Psychiatry's Division of Managed Behavioral Health and Addiction Psychiatry Fellowship Program. He is triple-boarded in general psychiatry, addiction psychiatry, and addiction medicine, and has special expertise in trauma, addiction, and administrative psychiatry. Over the past ten years, he has developed special expertise in designing prevention and assistance services for addicted professionals and their families. He is an active clinician, lecturer, and teacher, and has more than fifty published articles, chapters, reviews, and abstracts. In 1996 he was selected by *Baltimore* magazine as its "Best Doc" in Addiction Psychiatry.

Todd I. Muneses, MD, is currently Medical Director for Sinai Hospital of Baltimore's Addiction Recovery Program. He obtained his medical degree from the Tulane University School of Medicine. He completed his psychiatric residency and a postresidency Addiction Psychiatry fellowship at the University of Maryland Medical Center. He also maintains a private practice in the Baltimore area, specializing in dual diagnosis treatment.

James O'Hair, MSW, CEAP, is Manager of the Northrup Grumman ESSD Corporation Employee and Family Assistance Program. He has been involved in employee assistance and a member of the Employees Assistance Professional Association (EAPA) for twenty years. In that time, he has managed EAPs for the Major League Baseball Players Association, and consulted with the federal government and private organizations in Maryland, Massachusetts, Ohio, Virginia, West Virginia, and the District of Columbia on the subject of employee assistance. He served as manager for occupational programs with the National Clearinghouse for Alcohol and Drug Information, and has managed a consortium of small businesses in Massachusetts. In 1977, Mr. O'Hair also served as a consultant to Harvard University and the Harvard University School of Medicine and Public Health. He holds a master's degree in Planning and Industrial Social Work from Boston College. He is a Licensed Certified Social Worker, Certified Employee Assistance Professional, Certified Addictions Counselor, and has served as an adjunct professor at Johns Hopkins University Graduate School of Management and the University of Maryland Graduate School of Social Work.

Hon. William G. Schma was appointed Kalamazoo County Circuit Court Judge in 1987. He was elected in 1988 and reelected in 1990 and 1996. Prior to his appointment, he had been in private practice and corporate counsel. He has membership in various judicial organizations, and serves on two Michigan State Court Administrative Office committees. He has lectured at Western Michigan University, taught Legal Writing, and made presentations for Michigan's Institute for Continuing Legal Education (ICLE), Michigan Judicial Institute (MJI), Michigan Council on Crime and Delinquency, the State Justice Institute (SJI), the National Council on Alcoholism and Drug Dependence of Michigan, Inc. (NCADD-MI), the Puerto Rican Foundation for

Mental Health, the North Carolina Office of the Courts, the National Association of Drug Court Professionals (NADCP), and the National Institute for Justice (NIJ). Judge Schma is presently Presiding Judge for Kalamazoo County's Substance Abuse Diversion Program, a diversion program for felony substance abusers. He is a founding member of the National Association for Drug Court Professionals, and serves on the Board of Directors of Prevention Works, Inc., a community coalition promoting collaborative prevention strategies.

John Steinberg, MD, is a native of Baltimore, Maryland, who graduated from the McDonogh School as a National Merit Honors finalist. He received his undergraduate degree in biochemistry from Michigan State University with High Honors, and was elected to Phi Beta Kappa. After graduate work in biochemistry, Dr. Steinberg received his MD from the University of Maryland School of Medicine, and completed a residency in Internal Medicine at the Greater Baltimore Medical Center. He was then certified in Addiction Medicine by the American Society of Addiction Medicine. Dr. Steinberg currently holds faculty appointments at the University of Maryland School of Medicine in the departments of Family Medicine and Psychiatry. His teaching responsibilities include core didactic lectures on hypertension and hyperlipidemia for the Family Medicine residents. He works with both the impaired Physician Rehabilitation Committee and the Board of Physician Quality Assurance in dealing with impaired physicians, and maintains a practice in the field of general Internal Medicine. He has lectured extensively, both nationally and internationally, on cardiovascular subjects and on the interface of medicine and psychiatry.

Stuart A. Tiegel, MSW, LCSW-C is Assistant Professor and Director of Education in the Division of Alcohol and Drug Abuse, Department of Psychiatry, School of Medicine, University of Maryland. Mr. Tiegel also holds a faculty appointment in the Johns Hopkins University School of Medicine. He teaches Family Therapy to third-year residents in both medical schools. He has also conducted private practice since 1976, actively using interventions since then. Mr. Tiegel has trained at the Family Therapy Institute in Washington, DC, and was also on their faculty. Mr. Tiegel is an active teacher, supervisor, and practitioner in family therapy, addictions, and psychotherapy. He is a past vice president of the Maryland Society for Clinical Social Work and a member of the Maryland Social Work Rehabilitation Committee for NASW. Research interests and publications include substance abuse and family therapy, and the issue of loss in substance-abusing families. Mr. Tiegel has presented at national conferences on several topics, including physician/nonphysician collaboration in psychotherapy, substance abuse in families, and abusing families.

Penelope P. Ziegler, MD, was recently appointed Medical Director of the Farley Center, an extended treatment program for health professionals, located in Colonial Williamsburg, Virginia. She is an active member of the American Society of Addiction Medicine, and currently serves on their Publications and HIV/AIDS Committees. She is also an active member of the American Academy of Addiction Psychiatry, as well as many other professional organizations. Dr. Ziegler has published numerous articles relating to issues of significance to the impaired health care provider, and she has presented several papers at regional, national, and international conferences. Licensed to practice medicine in Virginia, Pennsylvania, and Maryland, Dr. Ziegler is also a Diplomate, National Board of Medical Examiners, and is certified in General Psychiatry with added qualifications in Addiction Psychiatry and Addiction Medicine.

Foreword

The problem is how do we get people who are dying, who do not believe they are dying, who fight the slightest inkling they are dying, to believe that they are dying and accept help which will save their lives? This question has always lived at the center of the tragic conundrum that is the alcoholic and other-drug-addicted person.

One of the early solutions was allowing addicted individuals to "hit bottom"—to lose so much to their disease that they would surrender and admit defeat, thus beginning the healing process. But in many cases, hitting bottom meant death, dementia, or other dire consequences.

Vernon Johnson introduced the idea of "raising the bottom" so that addicted individuals could make the decision to surrender and accept help before they had lost everything. Over the past twenty years, his method of teaching families about addiction, enabling, and intervention has saved many lives. More important, they were saved before the victims of the disease had lost everything.

In this book, the authors have extended Johnson's methodology to other areas of life where addicted individuals are threatened by their disease. They use experts in the fields of medicine, law, psychiatry, and social work to help those who are addicted see the reality of their lives and accept help for their addictions. This book will be a welcome addition to the professional library of any interventionist.

Paul Wood, PhD
President, National Council on Alcoholism
and Drug Dependence, Inc.

Introduction

Deborah G. Wright

You may be a physician, psychiatrist, psychologist, nurse, family therapist, school counselor, social worker, attorney, or judge. Your profession puts you in close contact with people who have alcohol/drug problems. Whether the person's name is Joe, Manuel, or Sasha hardly matters because people with alcohol/drug problems come from all ethnic backgrounds and income and educational levels.

You are concerned for the person because this is his/her fifth or sixth "urgent" visit to your office, each one prompted by some new crisis. During each visit, the individual seems more defensive, more earnest, and more intent on having you see things his or her way, offering elaborate explanations and excuses. Regardless of what you say or do, instinct tells you there will always be more problems, more visits, more excuses, and even more involvement on your part. It may even be draining your energies, and the time and resources of your staff. Experience tells you that little can be done to stop the syndrome, but your professional ethics demand that you try.

You recognize the pattern because you have seen it before. You suspect a drinking or drug problem. But how do you know? How can you help the person without expending more time, energy, and resources? Most important, how can you initiate the kind of conversation that will cause a *fundamental change* in this person's decisions and choices?

The answer is intervention, a process by which individuals, many of them in your profession, successfully convince chemically dependent people to seek treatment. These professionals become the indicators in a lifelong process of change which is accomplished through the surprisingly simple application of a little knowledge and a healthy dose of genuine concern.

Intervention is about change. Rather than changing the frequency or patterns of drinking and drugging, an intervention changes awareness, attitudes, and resistances in such a way as to initiate even more profound and enduring changes in behavior and lifestyle.

Although intervention may seem like a monumental task for which no academic or professional development program has adequately prepared you, *health and human services professionals are in a prime position to be change agents by helping dozens of their patients, clients, and colleagues to end the downward cycle of addiction and begin their recovery process.* Most important, you already have the skills to be a successful interventionist—a knowledge of the individual's problems, an understanding of the consequences of chemical dependency, and an ability to communicate with patients, clients, and colleagues. All you need are the tools of intervention—the words, the steps, and the strategies.

In July 1992, Rob White suggested that we develop an intervention handbook for medical, mental health, legal, and other human services professionals. It would be a compendium of the most effective strategies by highly regarded specialists in several disciplines who could share not only their insights and experience in working with clients, but offer revealing case studies. At the time, I was completing an intervention book for employers and another for educators, agreeing with Rob that professionals who had regular contact with the chemically dependent were in the best position to be interventionist. His idea was a novel one, an interdisciplinary approach that drew on the experiences of various methodologies to give professionals the best possible range of intervention tools. I liked it at once.

Rob, a respected employee assistance program director and professional interventionist who trained with intervention pioneer Vernon Johnson, is the kind of professional who sees people such as Joe, Manuel, and Sasha on a daily basis. He has helped several hundred public and private employees seek help for their chemical dependence. He knows firsthand the impact that professionals can have on a client with a hidden chemical dependency. Most medical, legal, and mental health professionals want to help addicted clients, but they don't know where to start. They want the ability to intervene in a way that strengthens rather than threatens the relationship with the client, is truly effective, and offers safeguards against liability.

Few people are more effective interventionists than physicians, nurses, judges, lawyers, counselors, and social workers for the following reasons:

1. By the very nature of their business, they are sought to address the kinds of physical, social, and emotional problems that are often caused by substance abuse.
2. The client already relies on them for accurate information, personal objectivity, and a guarantee of confidentiality.
3. Such professionals have the access to factual records and client histories, as well as ability to conduct assessments that can help identify chronic substance abuse.
4. They have factual knowledge of the consequences of the drinking or drug use and an ability to communicate information of a personal nature to the client.
5. They have knowledge of and access to reliable treatment resources, can make referrals, and line up assessments and intakes.

As an alcohol and drug educator and intervention trainer, I saw a second impetus for this book. Reductions in insurance coverage, public funds for health care services, and private funding of employee assistance programs have greatly reduced the availability of trained professionals to conduct interventions. If interventions are to occur, and if people are to receive help before their dependency progresses to a stage where they cannot be helped, interventions will have to come earlier and from those individuals who are already involved in advising, assisting, and treating people for problems which result from substance abuse—the health and human services professionals.

The potential power of an intervention to initiate recovery became obvious to me in 1986 while lecturing to a room full of addicts. These men and women, who ranged in age from thirteen to seventy, were just beginning a treatment program. When asked who in the room had "volunteered" for treatment rather than being intervened upon or forced into treatment, at first they all raised their hands. However, no hands remained in the air when asked, "Please put your hand down if you came to treatment to avoid losing your family, marriage or relationship; your job, business, client, partner, or fiances; or your mental or physical health. And please lower your hand if you came to treatment at the 'invitation' of your lawyer, employer, counselor or therapist, minister, or judge." When asked again who in the room had really volunteered for treatment, they all laughed and shook their heads. None had. None really wanted to be there. Everyone had experienced an intervention that motivated them to accept treatment as the least painful of the various options. It has been the same with every group I have questioned.

The reality is that chemically dependent people will not seek treatment unless confronted in some way with the problems caused by their drinking and drug use. They are motivated to choose recovery over worsening problems because of the actions of an intervening person or circumstance.

The key phrase is "motivated to change," not intimated, manipulated, or humiliated into changing—methods that have historically proven unsuccessful. The tools of intervention are relatively easy and can be found in many forms throughout the following pages.

Rob White begins the book with a comprehensive overview of the history of intervention—from its development as a family intervention model to its present application in medical, legal, and employment situations.

John Steinberg, an internist, gives an excellent analysis of the physician's perspective, including warning signs, how to assess symptoms using various diagnostic tools, how to initiate the conversation with the patient, and how to overcome resistances to referral.

David McDuff and Todd Muneses, clinical therapists, discuss intervention within the stages-of-change framework which allows the clinician to develop response-specific intervention strategies that are appropriate to the client's behavior pathology.

Jim O'Hair, Director of Employee Assistance Programs for Westinghouse, offers strategies for employee assistance professionals and supervisors to conduct effective performance-related workplace interventions, including intervention steps, conditions of continued employment, and obtaining professional assessments.

Penelope Ziegler, Director of Physicians Health Programs for the Pennsylvania Medical Society, discusses the development and design of impaired professional committees and various alternative models for peer and administrative interventions.

Jim Crowley, adolescent and family therapist and founder of Community Intervention, discusses approaches to early intervention for substance abusing adolescents, chronicles the methodologies of student assistance programs and teams, and offers clinical and treatment considerations.

Stu Tiegel, a family therapist and social worker, describes the benefits to the family regardless of the behavior of the addicted person. It is possible for the family to get well even if the addicted person is unwilling to seek treatment. Intervention can be viewed as a form of brief, structured family therapy.

The Honorable Peggy Hora and Honorable William Schma discuss the legal strategy of intervention. They describe recent changes in the criminal justice system that have encouraged judges to refer individuals to treatment in addition to any punishment. They describe the necessary elements for a treatment court and recommend guidelines for judges to follow.

Finally, the last chapter by Deborah Wright, describes the opportunity for intervention in the One-Stop Reemployment Social Services Center. It is a unique opportunity for these federally supported centers to identify and refer addicted persons to treatment. These centers can serve several agencies such as Social Services, Employment, Job Training, Food Stamp, Welfare, Child Protective Services and others. These multiagency service centers can share information and work as a team in order to assist individuals and motivate them to seek appropriate treatment.

Throughout these chapters, you will begin to see a similarity in the case studies, regardless of the age, education, culture, occupation, or addiction of the person in the intervention. Client reactions to an intervention are predictable, and the effectiveness of the appropriate responses is immediate and measurable.

Regardless of the methodology or the circumstance, four crucial steps are essential in a results-oriented intervention. They are best remembered by the acronym CARE.

1. *Communicate:* Confront the specific problems with the person. Discuss the facts and possible causes. Inquire about the possibility of alcohol or drug use as a cause. Discuss the stages of dependency and impending outcomes if substances are involved.

2. *Affirm:* Express your concern and desire to help the person as long as he or she wants your help, and is ready and willing to make a change. Listen to the individual's explanations, regardless of merit, and restate exactly what he or she has said in your own words.

3. *Respond:* Refocus on the problem at hand, the facts, outcomes, and the possible consequences. Discuss the options along with the specific help which you can provide.

4. *Enact:* With the person determine a corrective course of action and assist the person in following through. Do not give a mandate or a condition unless you intend to enforce it. Follow up with the person.

People with hidden chemical dependence will typically ask their health and human services professionals to address and resolve the symptoms of their problems (the broken wrist from a fall or the broken marriage from years of fighting) rather than the real cause (the chronic addiction to alcohol, medications, illegal drugs, or other substances). Most likely they are denying the real cause. Someone must tell them. Professionals who do not intervene on the chemical dependency run the risk of offering a Band-Aid solution to a life-threatening illness. Until the cause is addressed, the symptoms will worsen, affecting not only the individual's life, but the lives of many others. Symptoms, including behavior such as drunk driving, are more often the cause of death than the chemical's deterioration of an addict's body. Therein lies your challenge and your opportunity.

We hope that this book gives you the information you need to assist your clients. We encourage you to explore the other resources listed the bibliography. As professionals, we invite you to experience the reward that comes when a person says, "Thank you for helping me to find the help I needed. You saved my life."

Chapter 1

Family Intervention: Background, Principles, and Other Strategies

Robert K. White

BACKGROUND

Intervention became a formalized process with Dr. Vernon Johnson's development of "Family Intervention." For the first time, the stages of a well-planned, well-organized, and highly effective approach to confronting alcoholics and other addicted persons were identified and made available to clinical professionals, counselors, physicians, and family members. Many times, however, it is not possible to conduct a family intervention because the family is not available. As a result, other equally effective models of intervention have been developed which draw extensively on the concepts, language, and methodologies of family intervention. This chapter explains the family intervention process and its various applications and modifications as a foundation for extending the same principles to many other settings.

Vernon Johnson developed Family Intervention in the mid-1960s as a way to motivate the alcoholic or drug dependent person to seek treatment. The process relies heavily on the Disease Model of Alcoholism and Drug Dependence (i.e., chemical dependence) as its foundation.[1,2,3] Family and friends of the addicted person are educated regarding the disease and its treatment, trained in the procedures for nonjudgmental group confrontation, and guided through the actual intervention session by a qualified professional.*

Johnson, an Episcopal minister, developed Family Intervention as a result of a research study conducted in his church community to discover the reasons that alcoholics sought help. He concluded that the chief motivating factor was the buildup of a series of crises in several areas of the person's life. The individual's job may be threatened; the spouse may be ready to leave; the person's health may be failing; financial problems may be mounting. These and other circumstances eventually pressure a person to seek help. Johnson's concept was to create a situation where these problems should be identified and presented in such a way as to greatly increase the pressure, usually involving a mandate or condition and a time frame.

THE DISEASE MODEL

The intervention process is driven by a time imperative. According to Johnson, the disease of chemical dependence possesses several significant qualities that make it imperative or critical for individuals close to the affected person to intervene as early as possible.[1,2,3]

1. *It is a primary illness.* The addiction must be treated first before any other problem can be successfully managed. There may be several serious problems facing the individual (financial, marital, job, etc.); however, none of these problems are likely to improve until the addiction is treated.
2. *It is a chronic illness.* Chemical dependence cannot be cured. It can be successfully arrested, but never eliminated. The individual will remain free of the symptoms of the disease only as long as

---

*The National Council on Alcoholism and Drug Dependence (NCADD) operated the National Intervention Network (NIN) through many of its affiliates around the country. These affiliates provide certified interventionists to assist families and friends interested in organizing an intervention. The toll-free phone number is 1-800-654-4673. Interested persons can call this number in order to locate a certified interventionist in their area.

Other information about the NCADD can be obtained through its Web site (www.ncadd.org) or by calling 212-206-6770. The national office is located at 12 West 21st Street, New York, NY 10010.

he or she does not use the chemical. This is why it is recommended that alcoholics maintain lifelong abstinence from alcohol and other drugs.

3. *It is a progressive illness.* Alcoholism and drug dependence tend to worsen over time. The problems that are caused by the drinking and drug use will increase in number and severity if drinking or drug use continues.

4. *It is a fatal illness.* It is a fatal illness if left untreated. Many times the person will die from the behaviors caused by the substance abuse rather than from the deterioration of the body from the chemicals' effects. Accidents, trauma, medical complications, suicide, and violence are all examples of the wide range of factors associated with death from chemical dependence.

5. *It is a treatable illness.* The positive side of the disease is that it can be successfully treated. Drug-dependent persons that follow through with treatment achieve stable recoveries regularly. The estimates for successful recovery are dependent upon group-specific factors, but are as high as 60 to 80 percent in employed alcoholics that still have many of their social and financial supports intact (i.e., family, job, health insurance).

6. *It is characterized by denial.* Denial is a psychological process that serves to keep the chemically dependent person out of touch with reality. It is one of the most difficult aspects of treatment for alcoholism and drug dependence. Denial is caused by numerous factors which act synergistically, including distortions of memory such as blackouts and euphoric recall, psychological defense mechanisms such as repression and projection, and social factors such as enabling by family and friends. It is common for chemically dependent people to genuinely believe that they do not have a problem with alcohol or other drugs in the face of overwhelming evidence to the contrary. Family and friends become increasingly frustrated and angry when they are unable to convince the person that he or she has a serious problem. But, the person's memory and perception of reality have become distorted. Insidiously, the same disease process that is causing so much damage in the person's life is also preventing the person from fully recognizing it. The addicted person generally refuses the treatment that would arrest the disease.

7. *Enabling behaviors allow the disease to continue.* Denial also exists with the family and others who tend to secretly deny the seriousness of the problem and excuse it. Its most common manifestation is a behavior called "enabling." In most cases of chemical dependence, there is the presence of an enabling system made up of the people that are most significant to that person including family, friends, colleagues, or co-workers. They are usually acting out of a misguided sense of wanting to protect the individual, but end up enabling the disease process to continue. *Enabling is any behavior that prevents the individual from experiencing the consequences of their behavior.* Some common examples are: the spouse who calls in sick for the person who is really hung over, the co-worker who covers up for the person's drug-related behavior on the job, the family members who make excuses for the individual whose drunken behavior ruined last Christmas, and the parent who rushes in to bail the teenager out of jail for a drunk and disorderly charge.

FAMILY INTERVENTION

In a family intervention, the family and friends of the addicted person are gathered together, educated, and trained by a counselor. This takes place in two to three sessions prior to the actual intervention session. The addicted individual may or may not be aware that the family is attending these sessions.

Once the family is prepared and the appropriate treatment plan is determined, the actual intervention session is scheduled. Many times the addicted individual is not told the exact nature of the meeting. It is usually necessary to use some deception in order to ensure that the addicted person will attend. However, in some cases, the addicted person is made aware that they are attending a counseling session.

The intervention session itself is very structured, and the family knows ahead of time exactly what they will say and when they will say it. The process is designed to convey the love and concern that the family has for the addicted person and to prevent any display of anger or resentment. Each family member takes a turn to briefly state his or her concern, several incidents that have caused that concern and his or her desire for the individual to seek treatment immediately. Typically, the treatment center has already been advised of the intervention and the initial admission information has been provided. In most cases the initial treatment setting is a residential program which may be followed by outpatient group therapy. The hope is that the person will be admitted to treatment that day.

Consequences

The impact of an intervention is its ability to create and present the "crises" in the addicted person's life to a point where the person chooses treatment. If the person chooses not to go to treatment, then there are usually some significant consequences that go into effect. The spouse may be ready to file for divorce. The adult children may refuse to invite the person to family functions. The job may be terminated. In general, the family and friends withdraw their support (financial, emotional, and otherwise) until the person seeks help. It is important to note that these consequences are not done to punish the individual. They are usually designed to help the family member take some action that will protect themselves from the person's abusive behavior.

Part of the process of intervention is helping the family to determine what is within their power to do and what is not. The family cannot control the addict's drinking or drug use. However, they can control their own response to that use. The spouse need not remain in an abusive relationship. The boss need not employ a person who fails to show up for work. The adult children need not protect and rescue an alcoholic parent who refuses to accept help when it is offered.

These kinds of "tough love" consequences are not always a part of intervention; however, they are typically recommended. Many interventions have been done without any consequences for the person not going to treatment. It is generally recognized that the chances for success (i.e., the person goes to treatment) are better if there are some consequences included.

Goals

The primary goal of any intervention is to motivate the person to seek treatment immediately. There may even be a sense of urgency involved because of serious medical complications. Many times the family has initiated the intervention because of a current crisis that could be life threatening. Motivating the person to seek appropriate treatment therefore becomes the highest priority for any intervention.

There are, however, numerous reasons to do an intervention, even if there is little hope that the person will go into treatment immediately. Listed below are some of the *secondary goals* that can be accomplished, even if the person does not seek treatment immediately.

1. *The enabling system is destroyed.* This will make it more likely that the person will seek treatment at some point in the future. It becomes difficult for many addicts to continue their addiction without the support of their chief enablers.
2. *Family and friends receive basic alcohol and drug education.* When the people that are closest to the addicted person understand the disease, they are better able to deal with it.
3. *Participants are exposed to the local treatment resources.* The family becomes aware of and may even visit the local treatment centers. When the addicted person reaches out for help in the future, he or she will be able to act quickly.
4. *The conspiracy of silence is broken.* Just the fact that the family is able to sit together and speak openly about the problems that have occurred over the years is very important. Often there have been many incidents that were kept secret.
5. *The family is exposed to Alcoholics Anonymous and Alanon meetings (Narcotics Anonymous and Naranon for drug addiction).* These are the twelve-step groups that are free and widely available that act as support for the recovering person and his or her family.
6. *A contingency plan may be used.* If the intervention takes place and the addicted person refuses to go to treatment immediately, the family may suggest a contingency plan. This plan allows the person to "try it their way first." They may be refusing to go into inpatient treatment, but are willing to go into outpatient treatment. The family agrees to hold off consequences as long as the person follows through and does not relapse. If the person does relapse, he or she agrees to go into inpatient treatment immediately.

Limitations

The process of intervention designed by Johnson is a very effective means to motivate the addicted person to seek treatment; however, there are significant limitations that need to be understood in order to intervene successfully. *Family intervention is not possible in all or even most cases.* In order to conduct a family intervention, there are several essential ingredients needed. A group of concerned and caring people must agree that the addicted person has a serious problem with alcohol or other drugs, and that the person needs intensive treatment immediately. The caring individuals must be able to convey their message in a nonjudgmental, nonpunitive manner. This turns out to be a rather tall order for most families with a chemically dependent member. Since chemical dependence is a family disease that usually takes years to progress, the family may be angry, apathetic, or in denial. The following list includes many of the problems encountered.

1. The family no longer cares what happens to the person.
2. They are too angry and punitive.
3. They fear the anger of the addict.
4. They are in denial that a problem exists.
5. Some of the other family members are also chemically dependent.
6. The family is geographically dispersed.
7. The family is too fearful to risk changing the family system.

Some of these problems can be dealt with in the preparation sessions or in specific counseling sessions, but often they cannot. It is a mistake to think that family intervention can be used in every case. There are clear indications for its use and clear requirements that must be met.

Fortunately, there are many applications of the intervention process that are possible. The model of intervention developed by Johnson contains fundamental principles that can be applied to many settings.

INTERVENTION PRINCIPLES

1. The person has a disease that is causing significant damage in his or her life.

2. Denial is part of the disease process that prevents the person from fully appreciating the damage.
3. The person is unlikely to seek help on his or her own.
4. The people that surround the person can change the environment by destroying the enabling system and making it more likely that the person will seek help.
5. One of the most important factors in influencing the person to seek help is the sense of love and genuine concern conveyed by the interventionists.
6. Anger and punitive measures have no place in an intervention, and will only serve to increase the person's defenses and make it less likely that he or she will seek help.
7. Consequences for not going to treatment should not be designed to punish the addict. They should be designed to protect the health and well-being of the interventionist.
8. Individuals that require an intervention are in a great deal of denial and will need an initial period of intensive treatment such as a twenty-eight day residential program or an intensive outpatient program.
9. It is useful to intervene even if the person is not likely to go to treatment. There are many secondary goals that can be accomplished (see above).
10. Intervention is not "confrontation." It is a well-organized expression of genuine concern for a person that is sick with a chronic illness.

ALTERNATIVE STRATEGIES

Once the basic principles of intervention are understood, it is possible to intervene successfully within a variety of settings using different medical, legal, job, and professional strategies. In each of these settings, the process of intervention can be used effectively to make it more likely that the addicted person will seek treatment. The initial treatment option will vary depending on the level of denial, medical complications, and other factors. The remaining chapters in this book cover these alternative strategies in detail. What follows here is a brief overview of some of these strategies.

Medical Strategy

Many times the addicted person will come in contact with medical professionals. This could be the result of a routine physical or because of a hospital visit to treat a medical complication of the person's drug dependence. If the medical professional is knowledgeable about addiction he or she will accomplish three basic tasks.[4]

1. Make the diagnosis.
2. Tell the patient.
3. Refer to treatment.

In some cases, the physician can accomplish the primary goal of intervention by simply doing these three things. The sources of leverage in this strategy include: the sense of concern conveyed by the medical team, the weight of medical authority, fear of further illness and death, feelings of vulnerability due to sickness, and the period of enforced sobriety while in the hospital. All of these factors serve to create a "window of opportunity" where the individual is more likely to perceive the problem and accept appropriate treatment.

Examples

A. A patient that was admitted to the hospital for pancreatitis was referred directly to a residential treatment program from the hospital. The physician contacted the spouse and coordinated a bedside intervention with the help of the hospital alcoholism counselor.

B. A patient who had seen a primary care physician for a routine checkup showed elevated liver enzymes on lab results. The physician gained the patient's permission to interview the patient and spouse in a joint session regarding the patient's health. With the spouse present, the patient was unable to deny the drinking problem and was referred to treatment.

Legal Strategy

The addicted individual may come in contact with the legal system in a number of different ways. Probably the most common reason is for a drunk driving violation (i.e., driving while intoxicated [DWI], or driving under the influence [DUI]). Each state has its own set of criteria and penalties, but increasingly one of the requirements for the violator is mandatory exposure to education and treatment. Recent data show that individuals who are exposed to treatment are less likely to repeat than those exposed to punitive measures only. Judges are now offering many convicted drunk drivers the opportunity to receive treatment instead of increased penalties. However, if the drunk driver is a repeat offender who has had treatment experience, the penalties are much harsher.

Other points of contact with the legal system might include violent crime, drunk and disorderly charges, spousal or child abuse, drug-related charges, etc. In all of these cases, some form of treatment could be required by the judge either in addition to the penalties or in lieu of the penalties, depending on the case. It is important to note that any decisions regarding treatment may be independent of legal consequences.

In some instances, the threat of legal consequences may motivate the individual to seek treatment. However, an individual may not escape punishment for an illegal act simply because he or she was intoxicated. There are two separate issues involved, treatment and punishment, that may be dealt with independently. It may be appropriate to use the threat of punishment to motivate the individual to comply with treatment. But offering treatment should never be seen as removing guilt for certain criminal behavior. It should be seen as a sentencing option when there are mitigating circumstances, such as evidence of addiction.

Probation officers, attorneys, police officers, court alcoholism evaluators, social workers, and others can play a part in recognizing the problem and insisting on treatment. The obvious leverage of the courts can play a very significant part in intervention.

Examples

A. Driver appears in court with two prior DWI offenses and is mandated to attend residential treatment in addition to jail time.

B. Family member has tried to engage the alcoholic into treatment through several efforts, but has been unsuccessful. Alcoholic continues to drive drunk. Family member calls state police to alert them that alcoholic is drunk and driving. State police observe the driver and administer field sobriety test. Individual fails test and is charged with DWI. Later is mandated to alcohol education and outpatient treatment.

EAP Strategy

Most of the Fortune 500 companies and many smaller companies now have employee assistance programs (EAPs). These are free, confidential counseling programs for the employees and their families. Most of the cases that come to the EAP are related to alcohol or drug dependence. Most of the cases are self-referred, but a significant number of employees are referred by their supervisors.

The job becomes a very effective setting in which to deal with the problem of chemical dependence. Once the employee's job performance is affected, it becomes the supervisor's problem and as such, he or she can refer the employee to the EAP for an evaluation and possible referral to treatment. If the employee refuses to cooperate with the EAP, then the supervisor has no choice but to proceed with the next step in the disciplinary process. This may include suspension or termination.

Again, it is important to note that the consequences for not going to treatment are not designed to punish. Rather, they are designed to protect the interventionist. In this case, the employer has a right to expect adequate job performance. If the employee is unable to provide adequate performance because of a personal problem for which he or she will not accept help, the supervisor will proceed with disciplinary action.

In most cases, the supervisor is interested in helping the employee and wants to keep him or her employed. It is costly and difficult to rehire and retrain employees. The leverage provided by the job is very effective in motivating the employee to follow through with treatment. And, it is the more likely that the alcoholic/addict will achieve stable recovery if he or she follows through with treatment.

Examples

A. Spouse goes to a psychologist for counseling related to stress in a marriage that is caused by a spouse's drinking. Psychologist suggests that the spouse contact the company's EAP. Family member calls EAP for appointment. A free, confidential counseling session is arranged. The EAP had already been alerted of a possible problem with the employee by the supervisor, but there was not enough evidence. The family member's information confirms the diagnosis. An intervention is scheduled on the job with the following persons present: the EAP counselor, the company physician, the supervisor, the spouse, and the alcoholic. The employee is required to go to treatment and follow-up counseling is provided by the EAP.

B. Employee is sent to the EAP following a poor annual evaluation. One of the major problems cited was excessive sick leave. During the interview, the employee conceded that cocaine use had caused some of the problems with sick leave, but that everything was now under control and treatment was not necessary. The employee agreed, however, to go for treatment if the problems continued and he or she could not stop using (contingency contract). Within a month the employee had additional problems and agreed to go for treatment. A one-year treatment contract including group therapy, self-help meetings, EAP followup, and urine monitoring was signed by the supervisor, the EAP, and the employee. As long as the employee followed through with this agreement, the supervisor would not proceed with disciplinary action.

Professional Committees

Closely related to the strategy represented by the job setting is the committee for impaired professionals. Most of the professions now have committees established by either the state professional association or the licensing board that are designed to deal with "impaired professionals." About 80 percent of the cases that are reported to these committees have to do with chemical dependence (alcohol or other drugs). The remaining 20 percent generally deal with psychiatric problems such as depression or cognitive impairment.

The committees operate very much like an EAP in that they tend to assure confidentiality as long as the individual complies with treatment and does not represent a danger to others. The committees are staffed by volunteer members of the profession, although many now have paid staff who are devoted exclusively to this work. The state medical societies are the most developed in this area.

The function of the committee is to do the following:

1. Receive the report of an impaired professional from any source.
2. Investigate the report and determine whether a problem exists.
3 If a problem exists, the committee will have the individual evaluated by a competent specialist.
4. On the basis of that evaluation, the committee will design a treatment contract.
5 The committee agrees to serve as the person's advocate as long as the person follows through with the treatment contract.
6. If the person fails to comply, then he or she is reported to the licensing board for disciplinary action.

Professionals are no less likely to be chemically dependent. In fact, medical professionals are more likely than the general population to become dependent on drugs other than alcohol. The process of intervention and treatment is essentially the same for any group of persons regardless of their educational or professional background.

Examples

A. A pharmacist is reported to the Impaired Pharmacist Committee for the state pharmacy association. The complaint is made by a fellow pharmacist who has grown increasingly concerned about the person's deteriorating health and the discrepancies in the pharmacy's drug counts. The committee contacts the person and the individual agrees to meet with the chairman and another committee member. During the course of the interview, it is agreed that the pharmacist will begin a period of random urine monitoring in order to document that he or she is drug free. In a short time the urine screens produce a positive result, and the individual agrees to go into treatment, signing a five-year monitoring agreement.

B. A physician is reported to the hospital-based impaired physician committee as being overly tired, falling asleep on the job and slurring words when answering the phone while on call. The committee chairman and another member meet with the physician and refers the physician to a specialist in chemical dependence. The specialist interviews the physician and spouse and determines that there is good evidence for substance abuse, but not necessarily dependence. The physician agrees to outpatient treatment and urine monitoring. After a year, the physician has accepted that he or she is chemically dependent, is active in self-help, and has had no additional problems on the job.

SUMMARY

Family Intervention as developed by Vernon Johnson is a highly effective means for motivating the chemically dependent person to seek treatment. It is also a therapeutic process for the family members that participate. It is based on the Disease Model of Alcohol and Drug Dependence. Family Intervention requires specific education and training for the participants and may involve tough love consequences.

In order to use this procedure, some essential ingredients must be present. They must be willing to organize and educate themselves and confront the addict in a caring, nonjudgmental way. This is not possible in many cases; therefore, other strategies must be explored. The principles that are used in Family Intervention can be applied in a variety of settings that do not have the same requirements, such as: medical, legal, job, and professional settings. The primary goal—motivating the person to accept help—can still be achieved without a supportive family present and, in some cases, in spite of the family being present.

REFERENCES

1. Johnson, V. E. (1973). *I'll quit tomorrow.* New York: Harper and Row.

2. Johnson, V. E. (1986). *Intervention: How to help someone who doesn't want help.* Minneapolis: Johnson Institute Books.

3. Johnson Institute. (1987). *How to use intervention in your professional practice.* Minneapolis: Johnson Institute Books.

4. White, R. K., LeVan, D., and McDuff, D. (1995). Helping the patient in denial: The role of the family in intervention. *Maryland Medical Journal, 44*(6).

5. Bissell, LeClair, and Haberman, Paul W. (1984). *Alcoholism in the professions.* New York: Oxford University Press.

Chapter 2

Medical Strategy: Interventions

John Steinberg

Addictive illness is involved in as much as 40 percent of emergency room visits, 30 percent of hospital admissions, and 25 percent of physician office visits. Alcohol and other drug dependencies most often present as other disorders: accidental injuries, dizziness and falls, memory loss, aggression, sleeplessness, paranoia, and stomach and intestinal disorders. The primary care physician needs an understanding of chemical dependency and the ability to diagnose and prescribe appropriately. The alternative is to treat the presenting symptom while the underlying primary disorder progresses, or worse, to prescribe a medication which will further the addictive process. On the other hand, the physician is perhaps the most highly effective individual in causing a patient to seek the help he or she needs. This chapter presents information on warning signs, how to assess symptoms and initiate dialogue with the patient, the use of various diagnostic tools, how to overcome denial and other resistances to intervention, and strategies for appropriate referral, treatment, and followup.

PHYSICIAN INTERVENTION

Physician intervention in the course of addictive illness requires certain definitions to be made clear. First and foremost, to intervene in a medical sense means to alter the natural history or course of a disease. Anything that alters the untreated course of illness constitutes an intervention. Although the focus of much of this text will be on "structured" or "structured and coercive" interventions, from a medical perspective, this has a much broader meaning. Sometimes, an intervention into the course of an illness merely blunts its severity or alters the rapidity of disease progression. The ideal goal of intervention is to effect a complete remission or to achieve a cure.

As an example of intervention into the course of illness, we can look at malignant diseases. In some cancers, intervention achieves a complete remission. After a certain time period, typically five years, the intervention is considered a cure. In other instances, intervention into the malignant disorder's course merely establishes a temporary remission.

Other types of interventions into malignant disorders include palliative care. Here it is obvious from the outset that cure or full remission will be impossible. Nevertheless, intervention may achieve an amelioration of some symptoms of the disease, and may also extend the period of survival. Intervention into chemical dependency disorders is similar. In some cases, only palliative care will be possible. In others, a temporary remission will be achieved. The length of remission will be affected by both disease and host factors. In still other cases, a full and complete long-term remission will be achieved.

A physician cannot intervene into the course of chemical dependency unless the he or she recognizes that chemical dependency is a treatable disease. It is essential to avoid preaching morality to patients. One of the most effective methods of intervening in the course of addictive illness is to teach the patient a model by which he or she may understand the problem within the context of a treatable disease.

It is preferable to take an empirical approach. As has been discussed in an earlier chapter in this book, there are a number of ways to view addictions. An empirical approach provides results even if the explanation may not be completely understood. For example, scientists try to discern whether an electron is a particle or a wave. If an electron is studied as a particle, particulate properties, such as velocity, mass, or inertia can be measured. If the electron is studied as a wave, properties, such as wavelength and energy can be measured. As a wave of light, the electron may also be used to produce images. Electron microscopy is an example of an electron's wave properties. Thus, the issue is never completely resolved as to whether the electron is a particle or a wave. However, the way in which the problem is approached affects the manner in which it is resolved. Similarly, the ultimate resolution of the conflict as to whether or not an addiction is a disease may never be achieved. Yet, the approach affects the response. This empirical approach of treating chemical dependency as if it were a disease often enables the physician to intervene in the course of thé problem and to cause the chemical dependency to be resolved as if it were a disease.

One of the most effective methods of teaching patients that chemical dependency is a disease is to use the following set of concepts. Symbolism affects our interpretation of the events we observe. A symbol is an indirect bit of evidence that when associated with a particular phenomenon, gives us accurate information as to the true nature of that phenomenon. A policeman's uniform or a doctor's white coat are examples of symbols. When these clothes are worn by certain individuals, we can make reasonable conclusions as to the nature of their work. Nevertheless, the symbol is separate from the person, and outside of that context will not have any particular meaning in reference to a given individual.

Many symbols surround chemical dependency which tell us that it is a disease. It is treated in health care settings by health care professionals. It is recognized by every branch of organized medicine as a treatable disease. Treatment for chemical dependency is reimbursed by third-party payers in the health insurance field. If third-party payers were able to prove emphatically that chemical dependency is not a disease, no reimbursement would be offered. Instead, the debate centers on what is a fair price to pay. All of these symbols—reimbursement by health insurers, treatment in health care settings by health professionals, and recognition by organized medicine—are indirect but powerful bits of evidence that addictions may be treated as diseases.

It is also crucial for addicts or alcoholics to realize that although they are not at fault for their disease, they are responsible for their recovery. To be at fault for something requires specific intent. Simple intent is not sufficient. If a driver causes a fatality by striking a pedestrian, this does not necessarily establish fault. If the victim runs in front of the vehicle, this is an accident. If the driver of the car intends to cause injury by striking the pedestrian, fault attaches. In both cases, there is intent. In the first case, intent is simply evident in that the driver wishes to get from one place to another. In the second instance, there is intent to cause injury.

Putting this in the context of addictive disease, although addicts and alcoholics intend to use drugs and alcohol, they do not intend to cause harm to themselves or others or to develop addiction or alcoholism. Drugs and alcohol are used with the intent to alter an emotional state. Without intent to produce a given result, there can be no fault.

An additional concept is one of denial. We do not argue with patients who present to the hospital with pulmonary disease as a result of cigarette smoking. Instead, we treat their lung disease as an illness. Denial, or the irrational and illogical conclusion that one will be exempt from harm, shows us that fault and disease are separate issues. This holds as well for addictive disorders. Therefore, with a lack of specific intent, and the presence of denial, we can see that the addict or alcoholic is not truly at fault for his or her disease. Nevertheless, the addict must be responsible for his or her recovery.

One of the ways that this can be presented to patients is that although the health professional's responsibility is to render a diagnosis and to prescribe effective treatment, it always remains the patient's responsibility to implement that treatment. As a physician, I may diagnose a streptococcal infection and prescribe an antibiotic, but it will be the patient's responsibility to fill that prescription and swallow that medicine. Failure of a patient to comply with recommended treatment will result in an adverse outcome in the treatment of any disease. Therefore, I will absolve the patient of fault for disease, but will insist on responsibility for recovery.

The potential for recovery is enhanced when the patient understands that chemical dependency disorders are chronic diseases. Comparative examples are often useful. Arthritic disorders exemplify diseases which are more or less active on given days. Similarly, chemical dependency may be in exacerbation or remission at the time the patient is seen. Hypertension is an example of an illness where a cure is never the goal of treatment. Rather, the disease is managed, and the remissive state is maintained. Diabetes is an example of an illness in which the patient will be far more involved in treating the illness than will the physician. Chronic diseases are diseases which once extant, are always present. They may however be in exacerbation or remission, and to varying degrees, a certain amount of time must be spent by the patient to maintain the remissive state. Chemical dependency fits this definition. It is a chronic disease that may be induced into remission. The goal of treatment is to maintain that remissive state. It will be the patient who will put in the bulk of the time necessary to manage this chronic disease.

A basic definition of diseases may be presented. Chemical dependency, like other illnesses, is an abnormal state of health with specific signs and symptoms. It has a natural history which is typically one of progression and a specific treatment to which it responds. These related elements are found in most diseases.

OBSTACLES TO TREATMENT

It is often counterproductive to engage in debates with patients concerning the etiology of this illness. Some patients clearly exhibit a genetic predisposition to increased risk, and have family histories containing individuals with addictive disorders. Other individuals seem to acquire their disease and have no known genetic predisposition. For the patient, it is important to understand that chemical dependency is not contained in a pill, powder, or bottle. Rather, it is the interaction of certain substances with certain individuals. Once the disease state has occurred, it is more important to focus on treatment and management rather than to investigate etiology.

An additional obstacle to intervening in the course of this illness is physician-enabling behavior. Enabling is defined in the context of addictive disease as any behavior which enables the disease to continue in its active form. Physicians are notorious for being enablers of alcoholics and addicts. Sometimes this enabling occurs through minimizing the severity of the addictive illness. Other times, physicians will provide written excuses to enable patients to cover up their absences from employment which were due to drug or alcohol-related problems. This shields the addict or alcoholic from the consequences of the illness, but helps fuel the patient's denial and tendency to minimize the perceived severity of the disease. Another way in which physicians have been known to enable the disease is by repeatedly prescribing controlled substances which blunt withdrawal syndromes, thus allowing the patient to again avoid consequences of illness. The intermittent prescribing of a benzodiazepine to an alcoholic to blunt withdrawal symptoms in situations in which the alcoholic cannot drink is an example of this type of enabling.

Before a physician can intervene in the course of an illness, the illness must first be diagnosed. Chemical dependency is ambiguous early in its presentation. Only the later stages of addictive illnesses are easily diagnosable. It is useful to note early on, when chemical dependency is initially suspected, the findings that are observed at that time. With the passage of time and the evolution of a progressive natural history, the pattern of disease will become more clear.

DEFINING THE DISEASE

It is also necessary to have a working definition of the disease in order to diagnose it. One of the most useful and concrete diagnostic definitions of alcoholism includes the elements of (1) loss of control, (2) compulsive pattern of use, and (3) use despite adverse consequences. Formal diagnostic methods, such as the DSM-III-R, list the psychiatric criteria for diagnosing dependency disorders and addictions. Other diagnostic tools such as the Michigan Alcoholism Screening Test (MAST), the Drug Abuse Screening Test (DAST), and the CAGE questionnaires have certain point values to detect responses that indicate addictive disorders. These questionnaires are of different sensitives. The CAGE questionnaire is the simplest to use in clinical practice. Four questions are asked: (1) Have you ever *cut down* on your drinking? (2) Do you get *angry* when people talk to you about your drinking? (3) Do you ever feel *guilty* about your drinking? (4) Do you ever take an *eye opener?* This test is very sensitive but not very specific. Any positive response should trigger further investigation.

As to the initially mentioned definition of addictive disease, the three core concepts of (1) loss of control, (2) compulsive pattern of use, and (3) use despite adverse consequences need to be amplified to become relevant to a patient. A common response to the first criterion, loss of control, is that the patient will respond with a statement such as, "Most times I drink I can control my drinking." It is important to note that loss of control does not have to be absolute, but may be intermittent.

What is absolutely lost is the ability of the patient to predict when the control will disappear. As regards a compulsive pattern of use, the patient may profess an ability to "quit anytime." Again, the rebuttal is that many individuals can quit drinking or using drugs anytime that they like. The problem is that they can neither refrain from active use nor once stopped, can they stop thinking about it. The thrust of this compulsive pattern is not one of maintenance use, but rather one that reflects an inappropriate emotional investment in a substance. The final concept, use despite consequences, is necessary to secure the diagnosis. The implication here is that the patient has been made aware of adverse consequences directly related to drug and alcohol use which do not impede return to further use.

Rather than confrontational questions or direct queries concerning the amount of use, more subtle approaches are often of benefit. Instead of asking, "How much alcohol do you drink?" or "Have you ever smoked marijuana?" it is better to ask open-ended questions. Typical examples of questions appropriate for adolescents are "At what age do you think it is appropriate to allow people to drink alcohol?" or "Should people be locked up for using marijuana?" When you ask a philosophic question of an adolescent, pay attention to the length, the detail, and the emotional tone of the response given. A strong emotional response, that is indicative that the adolescent either has this problem or is affected by someone who has this problem. People do not tend to have strong opinions on issues about which they care little.

Another useful tool in diagnosing addictive disease is to focus on patterns rather than incidents. As an example, one DWI is not diagnostic of alcoholism, but is highly suggestive. Two DWI offenses are even more strongly suggestive. Three DWIs is essentially diagnostic of alcoholism. The first may reflect poor judgment, the second may reflect abysmally poor judgment, but the third DWI demonstrates the pattern of inability to cease using alcohol in a situation that is known to repetitively cause harm, thus confirming loss of control, compulsive pattern of use, and continued use in the face of adverse consequences.

PATIENT HISTORY AND SIGNS OF ADDICTION

It is also valuable, whenever possible, to obtain corroborative sources of history. A patient's story obtained with the permission of the patient or history volunteered by family members is most useful in helping to diagnose an addictive disorder.

Some diagnostic indicators are truly "red flags." A family may specifically warn you of a relative's alcoholism prior to his or her scheduled appointment. Some types of diagnoses will indicate alcohol or drug problems. Traumatic injuries are notorious for being linked to substance abuse disorders. As an example, a patient was recently admitted to a community hospital with rib fractures. The family had observed this person to be intoxicated and unsteady in gait prior to falling and striking his ribcage on a coffee table. With this corroborative history in the presence of a traumatic injury, certain laboratory tests were performed. Elevated liver enzymes and enlarged red cells helped confirm the diagnosis of alcoholism which was then presented to the patient.

Another type of warning that physicians may view as a "red flag" is a low tolerance to pain. A patient who requires an inordinately high dose of analgesic to control pain that is usually controlled by a much lower dose may be tolerant to analgesics and may be a substance abuser. Additionally, a patient who seeks drugs may often have a substance abuse problem. Examples include a new patient who requests a prescription for a controlled substance; a regular patient who begins requesting multiple controlled substances; a hospital patient who has a list of controlled substances; and a hospital patient with prescriptions from several physicians. All of these are very significant warnings and should lead to exploring the possibility of a patient's chemical dependency.

While there are no specific laboratory or physical findings which in and of themselves diagnose chemical dependency, many standard references will provide results which are highly suggestive such as elevated liver enzymes, enlarged red cells, telangiectatic blood vessels on the face, an enlarged liver, abnormal reflexes, etc. Again, whether looking at historical information or laboratory findings or physical findings, it is patterns and clusters rather than individual events or incidences which will help make the diagnosis.

A unique opportunity for intervention by physicians occurs when patients present with concurrent illness. When a patient is ill (for example an alcoholic who presents to the hospital with pneumonia), the patient senses a vulnerability. The physician may utilize the patient's perception of vulnerability to intervene and facilitate entry into recovery from an addictive illness. Fear and pain are good short-term motivators which do not work in the long term. If the addict fears mortality, financial ruin, loss of a family member, or any other catastrophe, this fear can provide useful leverage in the physician's attempts to intervene into the course of active illness.

The impact of medical authority when physicians intervene in addictive illnesses should not be underestimated. Patients often will respect a neutral opinion given by a physician. As long as this opinion is presented within the context of medical care, the physician may rely on his or her authority to impress the patient with the need to address alcoholism or drug addiction. It is important to be realistic with the patient and to avoid trying to bluff an addict or alcoholic. When bluffs are given, in most cases, the addict or alcoholic will call that bluff.

An additional caution needs to be mentioned. When patients are in a period of enforced sobriety due to hospital confinement, this presents a window of opportunity as well as a potential problem. The window of opportunity is that by virtue of patients' being out of their normal environment and in an area where the physician has more control, interventions may be facilitated. However, if addictive disease is not recognized, withdrawal syndromes may evolve which compromise the patient's health.

For example, a patient was admitted to a community hospital for resection of a lung cancer. The surgeon was unaware that the patient was an alcoholic. Postoperatively, the patient went into withdrawal which was inappropriately managed with narcotic analgesics instead of with benzodiazepines. The patient had a withdrawal seizure, became hypoxic, and succumbed to the pulmonary complications of an improperly managed postoperative withdrawal syndrome. This type of adverse outcome can only be avoided if the diagnosis of an

addictive problem is made prospectively and withdrawal is antici-
pated and managed appropriately.

All of the previous approaches have focused on the physician's
diagnosis and intervention of chemical dependency in individuals
who are clearly identified as patients. While discussed in more
detail in another chapter of this book, recognition of addictive disease in physician colleagues is critically important. Physicians must
understand that intervention helps rather than hurts. They should be
aware of how to contact a rehabilitation committee in the state in
which they reside. Quite often a physician will be among the first to
notice that a colleague is impaired as a result of addictive disease
and that the colleague needs help. Sometimes warnings are more
concrete. Any request by a colleague physician to prescribe a controlled substance should be a very suspicious indicator of addictive
disease. Almost all physicians will see a case of impairment due to
drug or alcohol disorders in a colleague during the course of his or
practice. Being sensitive to the fact that this disorder may occur in
one's peers as well as one's patients is necessary in order to recognize and aid in the rehabilitation of an affected colleague.

INTERVENTION MODELS

Having made the diagnosis of alcoholism or drug addiction, there
are several models for physician intervention. The first and most common model is simply to diagnose the disease and present this diagnosis
to the patient. This is similar to the fashion in which physicians intervene in any other medical illness. That is, to identify the symptoms,
present their conclusions to the patient, and then offer some course of
treatment that will alter the course of illness and hopefully ameliorate
the symptoms. There are certain basic approaches to presenting the
diagnosis of chemical dependency to a patient.

Addiction is a very sensitive issue, exacerbated by societal stigmas and prejudices. Misconceptions are common, both on the part
of the physician as well as the patient. Patients with a chemical
dependency disorder tend to have an inordinate degree of shame
and guilt, and physicians can easily be judgmental and derogatory
in their approach to addicted or alcoholic patients. Both of these
conceptions are counterproductive. The patient must be assured that

this matter will be approached purely from a context of health care. The physician must be scrupulous in avoiding the interjection of personal judgment when making this diagnosis.

The keys to presenting this diagnosis are to be objective, nonjudgmental, and supportive. To be objective means that the diagnosis of chemical dependency must be tied to objective findings, laboratory results, and historical information. This is a diagnosis, not an opinion. When the diagnosis is made, symptoms and findings should be clearly connected. The physician should illustrate the consequences of uninterrupted use. It is imperative to establish a direct, connective link between the patient's complaints, the laboratory findings, the objective evidence on physical examination, and the ultimate diagnosis of chemical dependency.

The physician must be very direct when presenting these objective findings to the patient. One method of presenting would be as follows, "The symptoms which you complain of, the laboratory evidence which I have found, and the findings on physical examination are consistent with a diagnosis of alcoholism." This leads naturally to the second element, that of nonjudgmental approaches. Because of their inordinate shame and guilt from internalization of societal stigmas, addicts and alcoholics are often very reluctant to accept the diagnosis of chemical dependency. Their misperceptions may include the belief that addictive disorders are hopeless conditions or that they represent some intrinsic moral weakness or lack of character. All of these opinions are erroneous. As the addict or alcoholic is sensitive to this issue, the physician must make every effort to maintain a neutral and nonjudgmental intervening approach. If the physician allows any hint of condescension or negative judgment to enter communication with the patient, this will render already difficult barriers nearly impenetrable. It is important to remind the patient that this is a diagnosis and not an accusation. Sometimes a direct supportive statement such as "This is a treatable illness which you neither asked for nor expected. It will respond to treatment, and I ask that you understand that my diagnosis was made as the most logical explanation which interprets the information at hand. This will not in any way affect how I approach you or how I treat you. You are entitled to respect and dignity, and addressing this illness will be necessary in order to alleviate the suffering that it has caused you."

A supportive prognosis should be given. Patients will not comply with treatment for disorders which they do not believe they have. Also, patients will not comply with treatment if they do not perceive it to be potentially beneficial in favorably altering the course of their illness. In most medical models, an intervention into disease follows the pattern in which a patient who feels bad seeks help and then is given treatment that helps him or her feel better. The pattern of intervention into the disease of addiction is to ask a patient who feels bad to feel even worse before he or she begins to feel better. This is because of the withdrawal symptoms and the change in lifestyle reflective of discontinuing active use of a substance after an addition has occurred.

Patients will comply with this request if they perceive that there is the possibility of a good outcome. They must perceive that the physician's treatment will not only ultimately alleviate their suffering, but will also carry with it a positive approach to the future. It is important to point out that of all potentially lethal chronic illnesses, few others than chemical dependency, if any, carry a 100 percent response rate. In order words, patient compliance with treatment is equivalent with recovery. Giving a supportive prognosis instills in patients a sense that successful treatment for this illness and the patients' subsequent ability to maintain a beneficial and productive state of recovery is entirely within their grasp.

The educating of patients continues to be successful in treatment of any illness. Use of the previously discussed disease model will often facilitate the education process. Thus, when the diagnosis, based on objective data, is presented to the patient in a supportive and nonjudgmental fashion, it will often be possible to enlist the patient's cooperative compliance with recommended treatment and thus effect an intervention into the course of active illness.

A physician may also intervene in the course of illness by participating as a member of the team in a structured intervention. For example, a patient was admitted by a physician for treatment of hematologic and gastrointestinal problems related to alcoholism. There was additional evidence of other target organ damage due to drinking, including a traumatic fracture. The family included many members who were recovering alcoholics. The physician sought to aid the family in intervening into the course of alcoholism.

A formal, structured, coercive intervention was led by a facilitator who was a physician trained in addiction medicine. As part of the intervention, the patient's primary care internist participated. The thrust of the physician's participation was that, regardless of any and all appropriate medical treatment, there would be no satisfactory resolution of illness nor any potential for full healing recovery unless the issue of alcoholism was resolved. Thus, the physician became an active participant in a very formal, structured type of intervention consisting of both a trained facilitator as well as numerous other significant members of the patient's family.

The outcome of this intervention was successful in that the patient agreed to enter specific treatment in a rehabilitative facility for the disease of alcoholism. From the professional interventionist's point of view, successful resolution implies the entry of the patient into appropriate treatment. This is different from the outlook of the physician, where intervention into disease process simply requires an alteration of the natural history to have some element of success.

With rare exceptions, most physicians do not make the treatment of addiction part of a general medical practice. However, it is entirely possible and appropriate for a physician to have an interest in and pursue training in addiction medicine to be both the facilitator as well as a care provider in terms of an intervention. As an example of this type of involvement, a general internist who is trained in addiction medicine was approached by a patient for the treatment of multiple bruises. The presenting complaint indicated the possibility of a hematologic disorder, and an appropriate workup was begun. There was no history or evidence of alcoholism at the initial visit.

Not only was the hematologic evaluation entirely normal, but another source of historical information was obtained. A friend and neighbor of the patient contacted the physician by phone and asked to speak to this physician about the patient's alcoholism. The physician played devil's advocate and attempted to dissuade this individual from making such a statement by challenging her as to the source of her information. When appropriate information was provided to suggest that alcoholism was a possibility, the physician asked to meet with this individual. As a result of this meeting, although the physician was careful not to reveal any information obtained in confidence, sufficient evidence was obtained that there were multiple individuals aware of the alcoholism. The patient's husband was contacted and her pastor requested to be included. The patient's employer called the physician and asked to participate. A formal, structured, coercive intervention was arranged. The physician was able to determine that not only was the hematologic workup unrevealing of patient's illness, but that the bruises had been sustained in traumatic falls.

The patient had forced her husband to leave the house, as he would not tolerate her drinking. Her three children were residing with the husband. The employer had threatened to discipline the individual should any further evidence of drinking, which was impairing her professional abilities, become evident. Fortunately, all of these participating individuals were willing to use their leverage to persuade this person to enter treatment for chemical dependency.

The intervention was arranged, rehearsed, and implemented. The patient went to an inpatient intermediate care facility for treatment of alcoholism. The alcoholism was induced into remission, and the patient has done well subsequent to that intervention. Although an exception to the usual role of physician participation, this case illustrates the wide range of possibilities for a physician who is interested in intervening in a very concrete sense with patients who suffer from alcoholism.

It is incumbent upon physicians as part of their responsibility to diagnose an illness, to document the findings that support the addiction diagnosis and refer the patient for appropriate treatment. Although physicians may not be trained in addiction medicine, they must refer the patient when identified as addicted or alcoholic for appropriate treatment by professionals trained in this area. In order to provide this type of intervention, that of referral to a specialist, there is little difference in this situation from that of any referral to a specialty provider of care.

First, the physician must be aware of the resources available in the community. This includes not only acute detoxification, which may be done as an outpatient or at the other extreme of intensity of care may be hospital-based, but also other types of providers of services. The physician should establish relationships as a referral source with at least one or two intermediate care facilities specializing in the treatment of addictive disorders. The physician should also have available the names, addresses, and telephone numbers of various outpatient providers of addiction services. Psychiatrists who are trained in addiction medicine, as well as addictionists of other specialty backgrounds, should be known to the primary care physician. The American Society of Addiction Medicine can provide a list of physicians trained in addiction medicine in any practitioner's area.

The physician should have some knowledge of self-help groups such as Alcoholics Anonymous, and be able to make referrals of patients or family members to appropriate groups. The physician should have at least a passing familiarity with random urinalysis and drug toxicology screening. The physician in primary care medicine should also be familiar with the prescribing of both disulfiram and naltrexone for use in alcoholic or opiate-dependent patients respectively.

Thus, just as physicians would be aware of providers of specialized care for ophthalmologic disease, neurologic disease, or any other area of illness requiring specialty treatment, they should also have an equally comfortable familiarity with resources for an individuals trained in the treatment of addictive disorders. Knowledge of this important resource base should be possessed by any physician in primary care practice.

The patient's medical record should accurately reflect the physician's thinking. When the physician has discussed the issue of addiction with the patient, there should be a record at least in summary fashion of this discussion. This record may be used later by the physician at intervention to show that the patient has agreed to try the physician's approach if the patient's approach has been unsuccessful. Therefore, a bargain may be documented between patient and physician, i.e., the physician has told the patient that the medical opinion indicates alcoholism and, if the patient disagrees, a reasonable period of time (such as three to six months) will be allowed for the patient to resolve the problems in the patient's own way. Thus, at a follow-up visit, if the problems are not resolved, the physician may refer back to this note and confront the patient with it, stating that he or she is obligated to fulfill the original bargain. In effect, the patient is told, "We tried this your way then; let's try it my way now."

When the primary care physician has intervened in the course of addictive illness and referred the patient for care provided by a specialist, appropriate referral also includes primary care follow-up. Physicians should be familiar with the ongoing care of addictive disease in the sense that they provide ongoing care for any chronic illness. The patient who has been successfully treated for chemical dependency is more properly thought of as having a chronic disease in remission rather than being cured. The primary care physician should learn about and watch for signs that indicate potential for relapse. The physician should teach concepts of chronicity, remission, and relapse prevention to the patient. The physician should also be careful to recognize particular dangers such as exposure to prescriptions of controlled substances. Above all, an appropriate dialogue should continue between physician and patient during long-term care so that the patient will be comfortable in seeking help, should the need for further treatment arise.

As the physicians learn to work with both recovering chemical dependency patients, as well as providers of addiction medicine services, their comfort and familiarity with this disorder will increase. This will have a positive outcome, and the physician will often be pleasantly surprised by how much they can learn about addictive disorders from the patients in the practice who are identified as being in recovery from these disorders.

In summary, the physician's entree or legitimacy for intervention into any area of a patient's life is to maximize health and minimize the consequences of disease. Addictive disorders are extremely common diseases, and it is essentially guaranteed that all physicians in medical practice will encounter victims of this disorder at some point in their careers. By learning how to effectively intervene in the course of addictive disease, the physician will not only restore families and salvage lives, but will achieve a great degree of satisfaction by virtue of observing the positive changes that follow the entry into recovery.

The physicians who are skilled in interventions will find that they are able to turn difficult patients into favorite patients to treat. Indeed, the recovery from addictive illness is one of the most dramatic changes seen in primary care medical practice. With basic knowledge and a set of easily acquired clinical skills, intervening in the course of addictive disease can become a satisfying and rewarding part of every physician's practice.

Chapter 3

Mental Health Strategy: Addiction Interventions for the Dually Diagnosed

David McDuff
Todd I. Muneses

INTRODUCTION

Substance abuse and psychopathology frequently co-occur in the general population and in mental health and substance abuse treatment settings. In the general population, individuals with mental illness are 2.7 times more likely than those without to have a substance use disorder. In addition, those with a substance use disorder, especially drugs other than alcohol, are 4.5 times more likely to be mentally ill.[1,2]

In mental health treatment settings, the strong association between substance abuse and psychopathology is also well documented.[3,4] In a study of 435 admissions to two inner-city psychiatric hospitals, Lehman et al. found that the lifetime prevalence of substance abuse was over 70 percent and the current prevalence over 50 percent.[4] Studies of the prevalence of psychopathology among substance abusers in treatment document similarly high lifetime prevalence rates for opioid addicts (86.9 percent), cocaine addicts (70.1 percent), and alcohol and other drug-addicted persons (84.2 percent).[5,6]

Despite the extensive documentation of the frequent co-occurrence of substance abuse and psychopathology, our understanding of these so-called "dually diagnosed" individuals remains limited. Weiss and Collins[7] discuss the complexity of the relationship between substance abuse and psychopathology, and describe five different ways to view it.

1. Psychopathology as a risk factor for substance abuse
2. Nonpersistent psychopathology resulting from chronic intoxication
3. Persistent psychopathology resulting from chronic substance use
4. Substance abuse and psychopathology co-occurring and interacting to adversely affect the treatment responsiveness of each other, and
5. Substance abuse and psychopathology co-occurring, but not interacting.

Lehman et al.[4] describe the heterogeneity of the dually diagnosed and recommend dividing them into at least two distinct groups for treatment planning: (1) primary substance abusers with psychopathology and (2) primary mentally disordered with substance abuse. He documents that in general, both dually diagnosed groups have more life problems when compared to single-disordered individuals. It is not surprising then that the negative effects of co-occurring substance abuse and psychopathology are documented in outcome studies of the dually diagnosed in mental health[8] and substance abuse treatment settings.[9]

Many clinicians describe the difficulty of engaging and retaining the dually diagnosed in treatment and suggest a variety of approaches to manage this difficult population.[10-13] In two previous papers,[14,15] we advocate the use of a developmental model of recovery to simplify clinical work in early recovery with relapse prone patients, many of whom are dually diagnosed. Previously we utilized the developmental models of Brown[16] and Gorski and Miller.[17] In this chapter, however, we recommend the use of Prochaska's and DiClemente's Readiness for Change Model[18] as a practice framework for intervening with dually diagnosed patients, since it has been empirically validated.

CLINICAL PRACTICE MODEL: STAGES OF CHANGE

As mentioned previously, several clinicians advocate a "stages of change" point of view when describing addiction models of recovery.

Prochaska and DiClemente[18] write extensively on this topic, and provide clinicians and researchers with a more objective way to determine a patient's stage of change along an addiction treatment continuum.

While these authors focus mostly on patients addicted to nicotine, their model can easily be adapted to discussions of patients addicted to alcohol and other drugs. What follows is a description of Prochaska and DiClemente's "Stages of Change" using patients addicted to alcohol as an example.[18]

Patients who have no interest in quitting and are unaware of any problems that their drinking may have caused are in the stage of *precontemplation* ("I do not have a problem with drinking, and I do not intend to cut down or quit now"). Most (50 to 60 percent) addicted persons are in this stage of recovery. When they do present for treatment, it is only when pressured. Examples include: a spouse who threatens to leave, a boss who threatens termination, or a court system that threatens jail unless treatment is pursued.

Patients in the *contemplation* stage (30 to 40 percent of addicted persons) are aware that they have a problem with alcohol, and are considering quitting. These patients, however, have no firm plans to treat their alcoholism ("I think I may have a problem with alcohol, but I'm not thinking of stopping altogether"). Patients in this stage spend a great deal of time weighing the pros and cons of getting help. Most patients, whether they verbalize it or not, have ambivalent feelings about treatment at this stage. Clinicians often label these patients as "unmotivated," "treatment-resistant," or "in denial" when in fact they are displaying ambivalence.

Patients in the *preparation* stage (10 to 15 percent of addicted persons) have an intention to change and exhibit some preparatory change behaviors. Specifically, patients intend to take action treating their alcoholism in the next thirty days, and have tried unsuccessfully to take action in the past year. An example of this behavioral change might be drinking one beer per day instead of the usual six pack per day for the next month ("I've tried cutting down a few months ago, but this time I know I can stick to it"). This stage is highlighted by some reduction in addictive behaviors, but no clear criterion for effective action (i.e., abstinence).

When patients are able to modify their behavior and/or surroundings in order to overcome their alcoholism, they are in the *action* stage. Patients in this stage have been able to successfully alter their addictive behavior from one day to six months ("I attend AA every day to help keep me from taking a drink"). Many treatment programs unfortunately organize their initial interventions on the assumption that most patients are in this stage. This shortsighted view overlooks the fact that most patients have not yet acknowledged a problem or decided to change.

Patients reaching the *maintenance* stage have achieved their goal of stable abstinence, and are working to prevent relapse ("I may need to take Antabuse now to help me maintain the changes I've already made while sober").

Since the focus of this book is to describe how to influence someone to seek treatment, in this chapter we focus exclusively on individuals in the stage of *precontemplation.* We outline and detail the goals of intervention with two distinct groups of patients: (1) substance abusers with psychopathology and (2) chronically mentally ill substance abusers.

As described previously, these patients are unaware of any problems their addiction has caused, and have no interest in quitting. DiClemente has summarized the reasons for being in this stage as the four Rs: reluctance, rebellion, resignation, and rationalization.[19]

Thus, we will focus attention on describing patients in each of the four stages as "reluctant contemplation," "rebellious contemplator," "resigned contemplator," and "rationalizing contemplator."

The "rationalizing contemplator" is not motivated for change because he or she has "reasoned out" why the problem is not a problem. A common example of this patient in the mental health setting is the substance abuser with depression. While the co-occurrence of depression and addiction is common and the depression is often drug induced,[20] these particular patients use depression as their reason for using drugs or alcohol (the self-medication theory). They view their addictive behavior as a "solution" to treating their depressive symptoms ("I drink to get rid of the sadness, and it works") rather than as a problem. They fail to realize that their addiction has led to problems that, more often than not, include the depressive symptoms that they are trying so hard to manage.

Although many mental health and addiction professionals will treat these primary substance abusers with psychopathology, a number will also have the difficult task of treating chronically mentally ill substance abusers. These patients typically have schizophrenia or bipolar disorder and substance abuse. Prochaska might describe this group as "reluctant precontemplators." For these patients the impact of their problems is not fully understood. A lack of knowledge keeps them from wanting to change their behavior. An example of this would be a schizophrenic patient whose daily abuse of cocaine and alcohol leads to missed appointments or medication noncompliance, which then leads to an exacerbation of psychotic symptoms and more drug use. For many of these patients, the possibility that these behaviors are linked in a vicious cycle is not considered.

Persuading dually diagnosed patients to acknowledge that a problem exists and that treatment is warranted is challenging for even the most experienced clinician. The remainder of the chapter addresses this challenge by describing intervention skills within a stage of change framework for two groups of dually diagnosed patients.

INTERVENTIONS WITH SUBSTANCE ABUSERS WITH PSYCHOPATHOLOGY

Depression, anxiety, and personality problems are frequently seen in substance abusers referred for treatment.[20,21] In fact, the reason for seeking treatment is often due to emotional problems or interpersonal conflicts rather than substance abuse. Since many of these individuals are coerced or pressured in some way into treatment, it is not surprising that many are in a precontemplation stage. With the view that substance abuse is not the primary problem, these individuals minimize their substance abuse due to lack of information, or they may rationalize it by blaming it on depression, anxiety, or interpersonal stressors. Others may completely reject the view that substance abuse is a problem arising either out of rebellion ("I can use drugs if I like; they do not cause problems") or despair ("The only pleasure I get in life is from my drugs").

Use of the Patient History and the Patient Diary

Since the relationship between substance abuse and psychopathology is complex and viewed quite differently by each patient, it is important during the assessment to objectively evaluate the exact nature of the relationship. Patients must understand that substance abuse and substance withdrawal can cause personality changes and mimic or exacerbate most anxiety or depressive syndromes.[21,22] In addition, patients must understand that substance abuse can also mask psychiatric symptoms. The most effective way to evaluate the past relationship between substance abuse and psychopathology is to take the history of each problem using *parallel times lines*. This technique visually and cognitively assists the patient and provider in making associations between each problem by analyzing the changes in symptom frequency and severity across time. The order of onset of the two problems, the effect of drug abstinence on psychiatric symptoms, and the influence of negative affects and/or interpersonal conflict on substance relapse can often be determined by using this technique. These issues must often be clarified before the precomtemplator will acknowledge that substance abuse is a problem.

Another effective technique for evaluating the substance abuser with psychopathology in precontemplation is the use of a *symptom diary*. This is easily accomplished by having the patient use a photocopy of a calendar that displays a complete month. For each day of the month upon awakening, the patient is asked to retrospectively record for the previous day any alcohol or drug use (e.g., A = alcohol; C = cocaine; H = heroin; etc.), and to rate his or her anxiety, depression, and/or interpersonal conflict using a 0 to 10 scale (0 = no manifestation of the problem; 10 = the most severe manifestation of the problem possible in any person). The symptom diary is then reviewed at each visit during a prolonged assessment phase of three to five visits or during each treatment session. Initially no aggressive attempt is made to gather specific information about the amount of alcohol or drugs used, since this often generates defensiveness by the patient.

The summarized information on the calendar allows the patient and clinician to carefully examine the relationship between the pattern of substance use, the psychiatric syndrome, and other problems. It is particularly effective with an intractable precontemplator to ask for predictions of the pattern of substance use or the frequency and severity of key psychiatric symptoms during the interval prior to the next visit. A brief trial of abstinence (for as little as one day or a weekend) can also be suggested, and the effects of this predicted in advance. The results of the predictions can then be compared with the actual facts as recorded on the calendar symptom diary. For individuals who initially resist or reject this technique, it is often helpful to ask that a significant other independently record the same information. Either the collateral's diary alone or the patient's and the collateral's diary can then be reviewed.

The symptom diary is effective for dually diagnosed precontemplators of all types (rebellious, rationalizing, reluctant, and resigned).[19] It facilitates the use of the three processes that Prochaska et al. recommend for shifting individuals from the stage of precontemplation to contemplation.[18] These three processes are: (1) consciousness raising (increasing information about self and problems); (2) dramatic relief (experiencing and expressing feelings about one's problems and solutions) and; (3) environmental reevaluation (assessing how one's problems affect the environment and others). The symptom diary allows a prospective and concurrent review of both the substance abuse and psychopathology uninfluenced by the guilt, shame, or embarrassment that often result from a review of the past. Without the burden of past guilt or shame, and through the indirect method of the symptom diary, the individual is better able to express and examine their anxiety and depression or assess how their interpersonal style is interfering with problem recognition.

The *rebellious precontemplator* is strongly invested in his or her substance abuse or maladaptive interpersonal style. The person is often help-rejecting and exhibits a strong need to be independent and maintain control over his or her choices in life. The symptom diary allows the person a way to list, quantify, and therefore control his or her problems. Many choices can be offered to these individuals in the design and ongoing use of the diary.

The diary can be used with *rationalizing precontemplators* to examine their assumptions about who or what is responsible for their substance abuse. If the substance abuse is ascribed to their anxiety, then this point of view can be discussed and analyzed by gathering several months of data.

Resigned precontemplators may acknowledge that substance abuse is a problem, but is not likely to change their pattern of use because they believe that their other problems are too serious or untreatable. They have no energy to invest in change because their depression or anxiety is too severe. By clarifying whether the anxiety or depression is caused or exacerbated by the substance abuse or is a result of an independent psychiatric illness, the symptom diary is able to introduce hope that change is possible.

Reluctant precontemplators lack critical knowledge that is necessary to initiate change. They may be unaware of the regularity of their substance use or its relationship to their anxiety or depression. Once they are able to appreciate the pattern that becomes apparent by reviewing several months of data from the diary, they gain the motivation and desire to change.

Case Study 1

M. J. is a forty-seven-year-old, never-married, African-American female, mother of an eighteen-year-old son, who was referred for addiction day treatment following a three-week psychiatric hospitalization for depression and suicidality. Despite more than a twenty-five-year history of addiction to alcohol and marijuana, and a more recent history (last ten years) of addiction to cocaine, alcohol, and heroin, she had never received any prior addiction treatment.

Her history of depression dates back to age thirty-three following the death of her maternal grandmother who raised her. Since then, she has remained chronically dysthymic and episodically on antidepressants. In addition to her recent hospitalization, she has been psychiatrically hospitalized on two prior occasions (ages thirty-seven and forty-three) for major depressive episodes. Each of her three psychiatric hospitalizations occurred during periods of heavy drug use (the first shortly after giving up marijuana and developing compulsive use of crack cocaine and IV heroin). There are no significant periods of abstinence, and substance abuse was never addressed as an issue in her prior psychiatric treatment.

Upon admission to the psychiatric unit, M. J. was depressed, avoidant, and preoccupied with suicide. She related her depression to an unhappy childhood, recent unemployment, and ongoing conflict with her live-in boyfriend (whom she described as physically abusive and addicted to cocaine and alcohol). Even though her depressive symptoms resolved during the first hospital week with abstinence, she had never seriously examined the full extent of her substance use, especially as it related to her acute feelings of depression or her chronic unhappiness *(reluctant precontemplation)*. While initially acknowledging her substance use as heavy (especially alcohol), she rationalized it as consequence of her alcoholic personality type ("an unassertive and avoidant wimp") and justified it as a way of dealing with her chaotic childhood and chronic dysthymia.

While in day treatment, a detailed alcohol and drug history was taken using the "time line" approach (see Figure 3.1). For the first time in her life, M. J. carefully examined the relationship between the changing patterns of substance use over time and her developmental and psychiatric history. She was able to see a clear relationship between periods of heavy drug use or changes of drugs of choice and/or routes of administration and the periods of more severe depression. In treatment, she began to actively evaluate the complex relationship between her drug use, personality style, and depression, and after several weeks committed herself to abstinence. She was confidant that she would be able to give up cocaine, and heroin but was not so sure that she could give up alcohol *(resigned precontemplation)*. She recognized that her addiction to alcohol had existed the longest and was strongly reenforced by the passivity of her alcoholic personality style. During the five weeks of day treatment, M. J. had three one-day slips to alcohol, cocaine, and heroin use. Each of these occurred in the context of reactive depressive dysphoria and unexpressed anger to ongoing conflicts with her boyfriend. To assist in the determination of her likely relapse triggers, M. J. began recording on a symptom diary her daily drug use, level of depression, any significant stressors, and the extent that her alcoholic personality style was active.

INTERVENTIONS WITH CHRONICALLY MENTALLY ILL SUBSTANCE ABUSERS

While the population of the chronically mentally ill encompasses patients with a variety of psychiatric diagnoses, our focus in this chapter is on those with the dual diagnosis of schizophrenia and substance abuse. We will explain why this group requires a slower and more structured approach to treatment than the group of patients

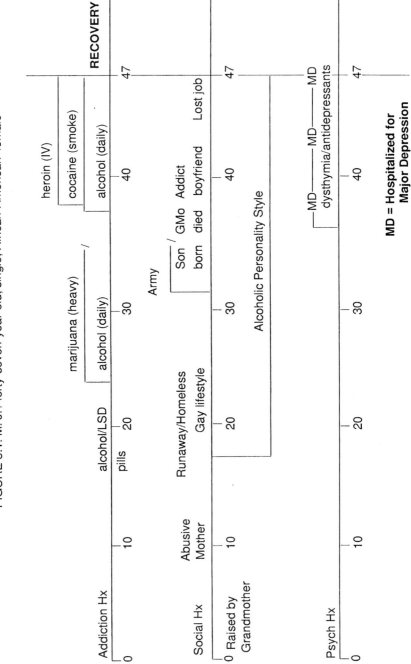

FIGURE 3.1. M. J. / forty-seven-year-old, single, African-American female

previously discussed. Some general concepts involved in the intervention process to engage these patients into treatment is detailed.

To better understand the process of engaging these patients into treatment, it is helpful to know the reasons why schizophrenics use alcohol and/or other drugs. Drake et al. summarize a number of contributing factors to this problem.[23] These include: (1) downward drift into poor urban areas where drug use is common; (2) misguided attempts to alleviate or self-médicate the symptoms of schizophrenia or the side effects of psychotropic medications; (3) attempts to develop an identity that is more acceptable than that of a "mental patient"; and (4) an attempt to facilitate social interactions. In addition, the same factors that attract nonpsychiatric patients to alcohol and drug use, namely the enjoyment of the experience and peer pressure, are also seen.

Traditionally, the treatment of schizophrenic patients with a substance use disorder involves sequential treatment: first being treated for their psychotic illness and then for the substance use disorder.[24] This approach, however, is not very successful. Problems with coordination of services develop because communication between the mental health and substance abuse programs is poor or nonexistent. As a result, the schizophrenic substance abuser often "falls through the cracks" of most treatment systems.

The literature in recent years has finally begun to shift from simply identifying this "dually diagnosed" group to offering practical treatment recommendations for the mental health practitioner.[25] Osher and Kofoed) propose a model of dual diagnosis treatment for the chronically mentally ill with the following phases: engagement, persuasion, active treatment, and relapse prevention.[26] In some respects, this model is similar to the developmental models of recovery mentioned earlier.[17,18] Both the engagement and persuasion phases involve moving the schizophrenic substance abuser from the stage of precontemplation to contemplation and preparation.

Osher and Kofoed stress the importance of these earlier phases with this special population.[26] The traditional goal of long-term abstinence from all alcohol and other drugs for schizophrenic substance abusers is difficult to attain, and leads to engagement failure and treatment dropout. Instead of focusing on abstinence initially, the therapist attempts to engage the patient in treatment with a series of concrete, short-term goals. Examples include: keeping appointments, attending a group therapy session, taking medication as directed, or even acknowledging the regular use of alcohol or drugs to the therapist. The use of these more realistic goals may help to engage these patients in treatment and persuade them to stay in treatment until abstinence is attainable and the long-term benefits of becoming drug-free are realized.

Key Elements in the Persuasion Stage

Carey[25] summarizes the important components of interviewing in the persuasion stage of treatment for chronically mentally ill substance abusers as: (1) it is nonconfrontational; (2) it views motivation for change as a dynamic state rather than as a static trait; (3) readiness to change can be influenced by major life crises and by therapeutic interventions; (4) building readiness to change may be a long-term process; and (5) key elements include creating discrepancies, altering the perceived cost-benefit ratio, and enhancing self-efficacy.

The key elements referred to above were originally described by Miller and Rollnick as part of their five general principles of motivational interviewing.[27] Using the schizophrenic substance abusing population as a focus, let us examine these principles in more detail.

The first principle is to *express empathy*. Here, the therapist unconditionally accepts the patient and through active listening attempts to understand the patient's feelings and perspectives without judging, criticizing, or blaming. In the case of a substance abusing schizophrenic, a genuine attempt is made to fully understand the positive reasons for using alcohol and/or other drugs. *Developing discrepancy* refers to creating in the patient's mind a discrepancy between a current behavior and a future goal by using a risk-benefit analysis. An example of this might be a therapist who points out a repeating pattern of homelessness resulting from the patient's dismissal from several group homes for fighting and being intoxicated. *Avoiding argumentation* refers to avoiding direct confrontation. While confrontation may be useful with primary substance abusers, it is usually detrimental in the treatment of the schizophrenic substance abuser. To *roll with resistance* means that reluctance and ambivalence are not opposed, but are acknowledged by the therapist to be normal and understandable. Using this principle with the schizophrenic substance abuser, the therapist would allow much more time to go from the stage of precontemplation to contemplation, since for many schizophrenics, drugs are one of their few sources of pleasure or their sole basis for social interaction. The fifth and final principle to *support self-efficacy* refers to supporting a patient's belief in his or her ability to carry out or succeed with a specific task. This involves changing the patient's perception about his or her capacity to cope with obstacles and eventually change. With the schizophrenic substance abuser, this support can range from reassurance about attempts to change to finding other solutions to using alcohol as a way to manage neuroleptic side effects.

By using these five principles, the therapist is able to reach the *reluctant (lack of knowledge)* or *resigned (overwhelmed) precontemplator.*[19] For many *reluctant* schizophrenic substance abusers, a lack of knowledge concerning the destructiveness of their substance abuse or the existence of rewarding alternatives to substance use keeps them from seeking treatment. In structured psychoeducational group formats, these approaches can be used to help patients gain knowledge about how substance abuse interferes with their functioning.

The *resigned* schizophrenic substance abuser has usually lost any confidence that change is possible. The functional deficits created by the psychotic illness have reduced self-esteem and self-efficacy and generated intense pessimism. Through the use of a buddy system (i.e., matching the precontemplator with an empathic, recovering individual) and by focusing on strengths and successes a sense of self-efficacy can be restored.

Case Study 2

M. D. is a twenty-nine-year-old single, African-American male with a twelve-year history of chronic, undifferentiated schizophrenia and marijuana, alcohol, and cocaine dependence who was referred to a public day treatment program after his thirteenth psychiatric hospitalization. When psychotic, he would experience auditory hallucinations and bizarre delusions of "rats" entering his body. M. D. also had borderline mental retardation and was residing in a local supervised boarding home upon referral. His drug of choice was marijuana (smoking one to two times per week), but he had more frequent access to alcohol (drinking beer and hard liquor three to four times per week). Less frequently, he would smoke (and sometimes ingest) crack cocaine.

M. D. could not understand how his substance use worsened his schizophrenia *(reluctant precontemplation)*. To him, the drugs and alcohol helped to drown out the voices and quell the frightening and intrusive thoughts. Prior to day treatment, he was consistently noncompliant with outpatient appointments and medication, despite having a supportive and active mother. M. D. also expressed frustration and pessimism to the day treatment staff after his multiple hospitalizations and poor response to medications. This pessimism made the initial attempts to address his drug and alcohol use futile *(resigned precontemplation)*. The severity of his schizophrenia and his active substance use led to numerous missed appointments or lateness to the day treatment program. His therapist also noticed that his alcohol use almost always led to the use of marijuana and cocaine.

The day treatment program began to intervene in a number of ways. First, M. D. was provided unconditional attention and support *(express empathy)* on a five-day-per-week basis. A behavior modification program was developed which rewarded him (money supplied by his mother and given by the staff) if he showed up on time. Random breathalyzers and urinanalyses were used to document and reward abstinence rather than to punish continued use *(roll with resistance)*. He participated in two nonconfrontive addiction education groups per week that discussed the various drug of abuse, reasons for using/abstaining, and the meaning of dual diagnosis *(avoid argumentation)*. M. D. also had individual supportive therapy that encouraged his attempts to change and helped him develop other coping strategies other than self-medication *(support self-efficacy)*.

Early in treatment, M. D. established an important goal of obtaining a job. After his motivation to work was strengthened, a referral to a vocational rehabilitation program was made. Unfortunately, this program had a rule that a patient who had a positive drug or alcohol screen could not be referred for at least three months. This policy was used to illustrate concretely how continued drug use could interfere with an important future goal *(developing discrep-*

ancy). This obstacle was dealt with through the use of Antabuse and an individualized treatment contract. An Antabuse support group was formed since several other patients were also taking the medication. Peer discussion helped to minimize the reluctance to use Antabuse and to strengthen the commitment to abstinence.

M. D. has now been in day treatment for three years. He has been abstinent from all mood-altering substances for five months and has a job as a volunteer at a VA hospital three days each week. The program has rewarded his abstinence with sobriety chips which are coin-like tokens that mark each month of sobriety (similar to those used in AA), as a way to reinforce his recovery.

SUMMARY AND CONCLUSIONS

Using a "stages of change" clinical practice framework, this chapter has outlined specific intervention strategies for use with two distinct groups of dually diagnosed individuals in a *precontemplation* stage of change. The similarities and differences in the intervention strategies with the two groups are detailed.

Substance abusers with psychopathology are either unaware of the extent to which their substance use may be causing or exacerbating their psychopathology or rebelliously invested in their addiction and its accompanying maladaptive personality style. The former need information about the exact nature of the relationship between their drug use and psychopathology, while the latter need to develop trust and resolve their help-rejecting tendencies before they will acknowledge a problem exists and can contemplate change.

Chronically mentally ill substance abusers often use drugs for pleasure, to fit in, or to self-medicate psychiatric symptoms or medication side effects. Within a supportive and structured treatment setting, they need to have the adverse consequences of continued drug use repeatedly demonstrated in a nonconfrontive manner. Only after seeing clearly that their self-destructive pattern is interfering with future goals that are important to them are they willing to consider abstinence and employ new coping strategies.

REFERENCES

1. Regier DA, Farmer ME, Rae DS, Locke BZ, Keith SJ, Judd LL, and Goodwin FK. (1990). Comorbidity of mental disorders with alcohol and other drug abuse. *J Am Med Assoc 264:*2511-2518.

2. Helzer JE and Pryzbeck TR, (1988). The co-occurrence of alcoholism with other psychiatric disorders in the general population and its impact on treatment. *J Stud Alcohol 49:*219-224.

3. Galanter M, Castaneda R, and Ferman J. (1988). Substance abuse among general psychiatric patients: place of presentation, diagnosis, and treatment. *Am J Drug Alcohol Abuse 14*(2):211-235.

4. Lehman AF, Myers CP, Thompson JW, and Corty E. (1993). Implications of mental and substance use disorders: A comparison of single and dual diagnosis patients. *J Nerv Ment Dis 181:*365-370.

5. Rounsaville BJ, Anton SF, Carroll K, Budde D, Prusoff BA, and Gawin F. (1991). Psychiatric diagnoses of treatment-seeking cocaine abusers. *Arch Gen Psychiatry 48:*43-51.

6. Ross HE, Glaser FB, and Germanson T. (1988) The prevalence of psychiatric disorders in patients with alcohol and other drug problems. *Arch Gen Psychiatry 45:*1023-1031.

7. Weiss RD and Collins DA. (1992). Substance abuse and psychiatric illness. *Am Addiction 2:*93-99.

8. Drake RE and Wallach MA. (1989). Substance abuse among the chronically mentally ill. *Hosp Community Psychiatry 40:*1041-1046.

9. McLellan AT, Luborsky L, Woody GE, O'Brien CP, and Druley KA. (1983). Predicting response to alcohol and drug abuse treatments. Role of psychiatric severity. *Arch Gen Psychiatry 40:*620-625.

10. Weiss RD and Mirin SM. (1989). The dual diagnosis alcoholic: Evaluation and treatment. *Psych Annals 19:*261-265.

11. Kaufman E. (1989). The psychotherapy of dually diagnosed patients. *J Substance Abuse Treatment 6:*9-18.

12. Minkoff K. (1989). An integrated treatment model for dual diagnosis of psychosis and addiction. *Hosp Community Psychiatry 40:*1031-1036.

13. Levy M. (1993). Psychotherapy with dual diagnosis patients: Working with denial. *J Substance Abuse Treatment 10:*499-504.

14. McDuff DR and Solounias BL. (1992). The use of brief psychotherapy with substance abusers in early recovery. *J Psychother Prac Res 2:*163-170.

15. McDuff DR, Solounias BL, RachBeisel J, and Johnson JL. (1994). Psychiatric consultation with substance abusers in early recovery. *Am J Drug Alcohol Abuse 20:*287-299.

16. Brown S. (1985). *Treating the alcoholic: A developmental model of recovery.* New York: John Wiley.

17. Gorski T. and Miller M. (1982). *Counseling for relapse prevention.* Independence MO: Herald House-Independent Press.

18. Prochaska JO, DiClemente CC, and Norcross JC. (1992). In search of how people change. Applications to addictive behaviors. *Amer Psychologist 47:*1102-1114.

19. DiClemente CC. (1991). Motivational interviewing and the stages of change. In *Motivational interviewing: Preparing people to change addictive behavior*, edited by W Miller and S Rollnick. New York: Guilford.

20. Anthenelli RM and Schuckit MA. (1993). Affective and anxiety disorders and alcohol and drug dependence: diagnosis and treatment. *J of Addictive Dis 12:*73-87.

21. Blume SB. (1989). Dual diagnosis: Psychoactive substance dependence and the personality disorders. *J of Psychoactive Drugs 21:*139-144.

22. Landry MJ, Smith DE, McDuff D, and Baughman OL. (1991). Anxiety and substance use disorders: A primer for primary care physicians. *J Am Board Fam Pract 4:*47-53.

23. Drake R, McLaughlin P, Pepper B, and Minkoff K. (1991). Dual diagnosis of major mental illness and substance disorders: An overview. *New Dir for Mental Health Serv 50:*3-12.

24. Westermeyer J. (1992). Schizophrenia and substance abuse. In *Review of psychiatry,* volume 11, edited by A Tasman and MB Riba. Washington, DC: American Psychiatric Press, Inc.

25. Carey KB (1995*).* Treatment of substance use disorders and schizophrenia. In *Double jeopardy: Chronic mental illness and substance use disorders,* edited by AF Lehman, and LB Dixon. Chur, Switzerland: Harwood Academic Publishers, pp. 85-108.

26. Osher FC and Kofoed LL. (1989). Treatment of patients with psychiatric and psychoactive substance abuse disorders. *Hosp Community Psychiatry 40:* 1025-1030.

27. Miller WR and Rollnick S. (1991). Principles of motivational interviewing. In *Motivational interviewing: Preparing people to change addictive behavior,* edited by WR Miller and S Rollnick. New York: Guilford.

Chapter 4

Employee Assistance Program Strategy

James O'Hair

Workplace intervention has become one of the most effective means of responding to drug and alcohol problems. The most common form of workplace intervention begins with an employee's immediate supervisor who employs what has become known as "constructive confrontation." This confrontation is most effective when a supervisor has diligently documented measurable signs of declining work performance. Based on performance measures, a supervisor can request that an employee contact his or her employee assistance program (EAP) to address those factors contributing to a decline in performance. Statistics indicate that one of the primary problems that causes performance deterioration is substance abuse. This chapter will explore how supervisors can assist in intervening with troubled employees, and also how to involve others such as co-workers, union representatives, family members, and friends. Special emphasis will be placed on employee assistance programs (EAPs) and their role in conducting interventions in the workplace.

DEFINITION

Alcoholism and drug addiction are progressive illnesses. Their destructive process can be interrupted at different points in an individual's life by confronting the individual with his or her behavior. This process of constructive confrontation is known as intervention. Intervention can represent the single most important event in an addicted person's life. Its purpose is to have the individual understand (1) that others are aware of his or her destructive behavior, and

(2) how their behavior impacts their respective lives. Intervention may be precipitated by declining job performance, family disruption or violence, driving offenses, or legal and/or health problems.

Intervention lies between prevention and treatment on the alcohol and drug abuse response continuum. It can be construed as any response to alcohol and/or drug abuse problems that is not preventative in nature and attempts to lead the troubled person toward a treatment or recovery plan.

Intervention

Prevention   (Early)   (Late)   Treatment

Early intervention involves activities that help to reduce the likelihood of problems occurring due to acute intoxication, and occurs at an early point in the history of the person's substance use problems. Late intervention involves identifying those who may be in need of acute medical care and treatment. The earlier the intervention, the better the results of effective recovery. It may also dictate the level of treatment response (inpatient or outpatient care).

KEY PLAYERS IN WORKPLACE INTERVENTION

Company

The responsible employer should establish a policy that calls for identification and treatment of people experiencing problems with alcohol and other drugs. This policy should allow for a rehabilitation process for those diagnosed with illnesses such as alcoholism and drug addiction. Guidelines for these policies may be influenced by federal regulations such as the Americans with Disabilities Act, Drug Free Workplace Act, and other drug-free workforce regulations.

Employee Assistance Programs (EAPs)

These are programs which employ professionals trained to assess, intervene, and administer appropriate treatment for employees and family members experiencing problems associated with alcoholism and drug addiction. It is often necessary to spend time consulting with supervisors, families, and others in preparing for a workplace intervention.

Supervisor

The role of the frontline supervisor is one that requires good documentation of specific performance factors. These may include absenteeism, productivity, and personal appearance (see the section titled Setting the Stage).

Unions

Organized labor can be a major supporter in successful interventions. As well as referring members, unions often participate in the intervention process. Because of the nature of workplace interventions and the role of unions with their membership, it is important to have union support. Where unions are not involved, they may enable the troubled employee to become more seriously ill. By not being involved, these unions may unwittingly allow inappropriate behavior to go unchallenged.

Benefits

The benefits manager or the third-party administrator is a key ingredient to the success of an intervention. Because of the growth in managed care systems, it is necessary to know in advance that the troubled employee will have coverage for necessary treatment and that this coverage will be supported by those managing care.

Setting the Stage

Probably the most important element to a successful workplace intervention is "setting the stage." This requires that the supervisor work closely with the EAP or interventionist to be sure that the documentation is accurate and can stand up to employee scrutiny. Documentation must support the claim that performance is negatively impacted. The following checklist should be addressed:

_____ Productivity (poor or erratic)
_____ Absenteeism
_____ Tardiness
_____ Excessive demands on supervisor's time
_____ Poor or problematic interaction with co-workers/colleagues
_____ Memory or concentration problems
_____ Changes in appearance or personal hygiene
_____ Need to blame others
_____ Withdrawal from co-workers
_____ Indications of other stressors
_____ Indications of paranoid or irrational thinking

Once this checklist is completed, dates and times should be listed for each item. The following model provides an expanded list of performance behaviors.

To conduct an intervention, the supervisor should first outline the measurable performance factors. Next, he or she should record any behavioral or other factors that reflect poorly on performance. Third, the supervisor should make clear what is expected of the employee, and establish a timetable for performance improvement. Clearly, the referral to the employee assistance program should be a key element, in addition to a follow-up session to review performance. Since most EAP referrals are voluntary, it should be made clear that the failure to use this opportunity to address contributing problems will lead to progressive disciplinary action. Model II provides a clear step-by-step approach for talking with troubled employees.

MODEL I: BEHAVIORS CHECKLIST

Early Warning Signs Are the Most Helpful

Job Performance

_____ Missed deadlines
_____ Errors due to inattention or poor judgment

_____ Spasmodic work pace: alternating periods of unusually high and low work output by a previously steady employee

_____ Lapses of attention, with increased inability to concentrate

_____ Occasional complaints from fellow employees or individuals outside the unit

_____ Elaborate and improbable alibis for work deficiencies

_____ Confusion and increasing difficulty in handling assignments

_____ A high accident rate both on and off the job

_____ Blames others for job performance deficiencies

_____ Complaints of being treated unfairly

Attendance

_____ Absence without leave

_____ Absence from post without good reason

_____ Excessive sick leave

_____ Absence on Mondays and/or Friday, before and after holidays, and the day after payday

_____ Repeated absence for prolonged period of time (two to four days or five to ten days)

_____ Excessive tardiness (usually thirty minutes to one hour)

_____ Late arrival and/or early departure from work

_____ Long lunch hours

_____ Elaborate, increasingly improbable, and often bizarre excuses for absences

General Behavior

_____ Complaints from fellow workers

_____ Overreaction to real or imagined criticism

_____ Avoidance of associates

_____ Undependable statements

_____ Exaggerated work accomplishment—increased tendency to try to "look good" to the supervisor

_____ Grandiose, aggressive, and/or belligerent behavior
_____ Unreasonable resentment
_____ Evidence of financial problems, including borrowing from co-workers
_____ Domestic problems interfering with work
_____ Deterioration of personal appearance and hygiene
_____ Apparent loss of ethical values
_____ Excessive use of telephone for personal business
_____ Mood changes during the day
_____ Complaints of not feeling well
_____ Claims of getting help for various personal problems without improving job performance
_____ Inappropriate request for outstanding recognition of medi-ocre job performance
_____ Inability to accept criticism or feedback on behavior problems
_____ Excessive apologizing for work deficiencies without cor-recting problematic behavior

MODEL II:
TALKING WITH TROUBLED EMPLOYEES

1. Describe the job performance in detail and refer to specific dates, times, events, of observed behavior. Do not criticize; rather concentrate on the unacceptable behavior. For example, "Beth, in the past month, your productivity has declined nota-bly. You're falling behind on the filing and you've missed agreed-upon deadlines in completing three of the last four assignments I've given you. You've also been absent from work four days this month (6/2, 6/10, 6/16, and 6/18). I'm concerned about your absences and their effect on your job."

2. State why you are concerned about the employee's behavior. For example: "Beth, last year you missed only one deadline all year, and had no absences from work. I'm concerned about

---

"Arlington Hospital Performance Based Intervention Model," D. Feerst, Arlington, VA 1994. Reprinted with permission.

what's happened to you in the last month—four days absent for no apparent reason."

3. Ask for reasons for the performance problem. Be empathetic to the employee's reaction and listen to the reasons the employee gives you. For example: "Beth, I know it's uncomfortable to hear this feedback from me, but until recently you've had an excellent record. I'm concerned that something is happening to you that's affecting your performance in a very negative manner."

4. Indicate that the problem must be solved, and ask for ideas in how to solve the problem. For example: "Beth, your productivity and attendance must improve. You can't continue to miss time from work. What can we do to help you meet these objectives? What are your ideas?"

5. Discuss the reasons/ideas that you and the employee have raised. The reasons for the performance problem can be strictly job-related, such as boredom with work, lack of training, or inability to handle difficult work. Other conditions affecting the employee, such as drug or alcohol dependency, financial problems, family crisis, etc., can be best handled by referral to the EAP.

The confrontation should take place in a private area or office, away from distraction. In order to separate the EAP from this confrontation based on performance, the constructive confrontation would normally not include the direct presence of the EAP counselor. In some unionized settings, it would, however, be appropriate for the union representative to be present for this confrontation. Use of the EAP in this case often will provide the employee with a grace period to address his or her personal, drug, or alcohol problem. In order to ensure that the employee sees the counselor as directed, the appointment should already be scheduled and occur as soon after the confrontation as possible. This will prevent the employee from having to dwell on the outcome of this session, changing his or her mind, or even forgetting the scheduled appointment.

The following checklist may be helpful in conducting a meeting with a troubled employee.

INTERVENTION CHECKLIST

Pre-Meeting Planning

1. Before confronting the employee, meet with other involved managers and be in agreement on: (a) the format of the intervention, (b) the seriousness of job performance problems, attendance problems, attitude problems, or other unacceptable behavior, and (c) the job actions you are ready to take.

2. Before meeting with the employee, arrange an appointment for the evaluation of the employee with a treatment center or EAP provider. Plan this appointment for about one hour after your intervention with the employee. If the employee agrees to an evaluation, he/she will be going directly to the evaluation site.

3. Intervenionists should have the authority to terminate the employee. Interventionists must be in agreement that the job performance problems warrant the agreed-upon job action. Addicted employees will seldom seek help unless they perceive that their job is in jeopardy or that other very serious job action is imminent.

Intervention Steps

4. It is usually best if the other upper management representative, rather than the employee's direct supervisor, leads the intervention. The process should start by explaining to the employee his/her responsibilities and how they have not been met. The employee should be told what is wrong, that the problems have continued, and that they are serious, etc. Use the behaviors checklist (attached) to help you recall all job performance deficiencies. Make it clear that this is a "day of action" and that you are planning to terminate the employee today.

5. After telling the employee the company believes termination is appropriate for the job performance problems, tell the employee that the company is willing to hold the decision in abeyance under one condition. Then pause.

6. That condition is this: If the employee believes job perfor-

mance problems are possibly the result of alcohol or drug use, you would be willing to allow the employee to visit with a professional, get an assessment, and receive help. If the employee does not think that alcohol or drugs are possibly contributing to the job problems and does not want to go for an assessment, then the agreed-upon job action will be taken.

7. If the employee would like an assessment, ask the employee to: (a) sign a release at the evaluation, (b) see a professional you have already consulted with, and (c) follow through with whatever is recommended by the professional.

8. Tell the employee that if he or she decides to go for an assessment, the company will support him or her 100 percent. If treatment is recommended, it will not threaten his or her job or promotional opportunities, and that appropriate time off work will be allowed (according to company policy) as long as the employee participates in the prescribed treatment program.

Post-Intervention Follow-Up Steps

9. If necessary, escort the employee to the prearranged appointment. Remind the employee that:
   a. This is his or her choice—he or she is not being required to go and you are not giving a diagnosis. He or she is going for an interview because he or she believes a problem exists and you are providing an opportunity to get help.
   b. You will only accept what the professional recommends, not what the employee thinks that he or she should do about the drinking or drug problem.
   c. He or she is agreeing to sign a release as part of the contract so the professional can talk with you.
   d. If the employee comes to the interview and refuses to cooperate or is not diagnosed as having an alcohol or drug problem, he or she will be subject to termination based on the job performance problems that you already discussed.
   e. This whole process is strictly confidential, and his/her personnel file will not include information about alcohol or drug problems, addiction treatment, etc.

One Last Chance

10. If the employee decides against an assessment, ask again whether this is really what he or she wants to do. If the employee still refuses, dismiss the employee for the rest of the day and ask him or her to think about it overnight and let you know, no later than tomorrow morning, what his or her decision is. Tell the employee that after this time, it will be too late. (This strategy may allow the employee an opportunity to grasp the seriousness of his or her problem and "calm down" enough to make a positive decision to seek help.)

HELPFUL HINTS

Timing. The best time to confront the employee is right after a work incident where a "perceived crisis" provides a sense of urgency, seriousness, and resolve. This will minimize employee defensiveness, make the fear of termination more real, and thus enhance the employee's motivation later when the offer for treatment is given.

Do not get involved in a discussion with the employee about whether or not he or she is an alcoholic/addict. That is up to the professional—not the employer or you.

Do not confront the employee on a Friday unless absolutely unavoidable. It is better to confront earlier in the work week to allow for time to deal with any difficulties following the confrontation.

The following case study illustrates the supervisory intervention based on performance, followed by an EAP referral.

Case Study 1: Ron

Ron is a successful technician with over sixteen years of employment with our company. Recently Ron's performance and attendance at work has declined. In reviewing his attendance records, he uses his vacation often on a Friday following paydays. These vacation days are typically called in on the days they are taken. His supervisor has asked Ron to schedule his vacation in advance to avoid placing undue work pressure on his co-workers. Recently Ron has been seen falling asleep at his work station and in meetings. His co-workers have expressed concern for Ron because of this. Ron has indicated that he has had medical tests to determine why his sleep patterns have been so disturbed.

A broader profile of Ron shows a dedicated employee who has excelled in athletics and has participated in corporate competition representing the company. He appears to have a stable home life with a wife and young child. Ron's supervisor has seen the decline in his performance and contacts the employee assistance program (EAP) for advice. The recommendation made to Ron's supervisor is to confront Ron on his performance and recommend he attend a session at the EAP office. An appointment is made for Ron and given to his supervisor so he can hand this to Ron when he confronts him on his declining performance.

Ron, who is also a union representative, is suspicious at first. He knows his supervisor, and feels he is setting him up for further disciplinary action. Ron also talks to some of his co-workers who have used the EAP. He agrees to go to the appointment.

Ron presents himself as a healthy, confident, articulate employee to the EAP. A thorough personal, medical, and social history is done. Ron is asked about current or past alcohol and drug use. He denies any drug use and indicates occasional alcohol use around holidays or special occasions. When confronted about any disruptions to sleep, he indicates he sleeps only four hours a night, and has had problems with falling asleep on his feet at work. We address any safety concerns or other problems such as concentration. We also ask if he has been tested for anemia or other blood-related disorders that may impact his ability to stay awake. We ask Ron when he last received a physical examination, and request a release to speak to his doctor. Finally, we set up another appointment for the following week.

At the next appointment, we focus on finances, which Ron indicates has been a problem for his family. I also ask Ron if it would be possible to speak to his wife. Ron is reluctant, then goes on to tell me he and his wife are no longer living together and that he has been staying with another woman. Again, I ask Ron about any drug use. He becomes defensive and asks if I don't believe what he previously told me. I said, "Ron I can only assume you are telling me the truth." I pursue the issue of falling asleep at work. I then tell him that it is common for people on certain drugs, such as cocaine, etc., to experience problems staying awake, a condition referred to as nodding.

Ron asks if he can tell me something in private. I assure Ron that all we talk about is private. Ron confides that he has been using cocaine for the past few years, and that recently his use has increased. He then says that he often would spend most of the money he made on drugs and took on a second job. When I asked again about his sleep patterns, he described a feeling of agitation that would persist and make it difficult for him to sleep and that he sometimes would use alcohol to get to sleep.

Ron and I talk at some length about the cycle of addiction and he agrees to be evaluated for treatment. We set the appointment up at the treatment program that day and ask a recovering co-worker to drive Ron to the appointment at lunch time. Arrangements are made to have Ron admitted for detoxification and then admitted to the treatment program.

Ron has since completed an intensive out-patient treatment program and has spent two years clean and sober. Today he helps other employees who feel they have their life together like he did when he first was confronted by co-workers and his supervisor.

ROLE OF EAPS IN FAMILY INTERVENTION

For many individuals, a key support system is the family. As a consequence, the impact of the family or family member as an interventionist with the alcoholic or drug addict may represent the most significant element of a successful intervention. The role of the family member often follows a precipitating drug- or alcohol-related problem (e.g., drunk driving arrest, suspension or job loss, legal problems, or illness).

Alcoholism and drug addiction increasingly is being viewed as a family illness, an illness characterized by the development of reactive patterns of interaction. These interaction patterns within a family may allow alcohol and drug abuse to progress toward later and more life-endangering stages. This may cause mounting stress to be placed on the family's already strained relationships. As the relationships deteriorate, the family members may feel a sense of guilt, alienation, isolation, and hopelessness.

Family intervention at this point is often the most effective means of breaking this destructive illness pattern. Family members who are included in most EAP service populations can contact their spouse's or parent's company EAP and seek assistance. The family member will be asked to discuss the presenting problem and how it is impacting their lives. Once it is determined that the primary problem is alcoholism or drug addiction, the family members are asked to meet with the employee assistance program counselor. At this meeting, the family is given their options. Clearly, if the person experiencing the problem is in denial, which is most commonly the case, a family intervention may be appropriate. Assuming the individual has not experienced serious impact on his or her job performance, the following steps will occur:

- A meeting will be set up with an interventionist. (This will often be someone other than the EAP counselor.)
- The interventionist will meet regularly with as many family members and others deemed appropriate to take part in the intervention.
- Each participant will plan a script that they can use when meeting with the troubled family member (see chapter on family intervention for steps to follow and what should and should not be said by intervention participants).
- The EAP counselor may want to participate as a cofacilitator and address questions raised about benefit coverage, company policy or management support.

The following case study may help in understanding how employer-assisted family intervention occurs.

Case Study 2: John

John is a senior manager for an engineering division. Over the years he has been on a fast-track beginning with a successful career following graduation from a prestigious engineering school. John's father, who was also an engineer, died at the age of fifty-one from an apparent heart attack just before John's graduation. John's first job was as an electrical project engineer. He has had increasing responsibility, challenges, and compensation in his nearly thirty years with the same company.

Recently John's oldest son Richard became concerned about John's change in behavior and increasing absence from the family. John married at twenty-five years of age and was married for twenty-two years to the same woman. They had four children. At the age of forty-seven, John's wife Helen became ill and was diagnosed with an inoperable brain tumor. Within six months, she died. John was devastated, all of his children with the exception of the youngest, sixteen-year-old Fran, were grown and on their own.

During the subsequent four-year period, John became more and more distant from his family. Though he continued to work, and on the surface appeared to contribute to projects, he became more unreliable. John began to drink heavily. At first, management was very understanding because of the sudden death of his wife. However, as time went on and John's drinking became progressively out of control, his management lost confidence in him. His sons became more distant and seemed to lose the father-and-son relationships they once had.

Although Richard did not know what to do, he had recently heard about alcoholism and the family, and he recognized similarities in his own family. He read a presentation made to a local business organization by the director of the employee assistance program for his father's company. Richard called the phone number and inquired as to what the company could do to help people who suspected their father may have a problem. Richard would not give his last name for fear that this would affect his father's career. For the next month, Richard would call and the intervention process was described to him. Finally, Tom, a childhood friend of Richard's father, called the EAP. He had known John through grade school, high school, and college. Tom indicated on the phone that he had been in recovery for ten years. It was during that conversation that a meeting was set up with Tom and Richard. We then planned the intervention. I put Richard in touch with Mary, an interventionist affiliated with a treatment center we had chosen for John. We selected this center because of the make-up of their staff and past success with company management. Following a month of meetings with family members and Tom, we planned a date and place for the intervention.

The intervention took place at a nearby hotel on a Tuesday night. John was coming back from vacation at the beach with a woman he had been seeing. The family chose not to include John's female friend because alcohol was a major common ground for them and she had little contact with the family. John was about an hour late, but when he did arrive at the hotel, he found his sister, three sons, daughter, Tom, the interventionist, and myself.

At the intervention, each family member made an emotional presentation expressing their love for John and how his drinking personally affected them. John was still resistant. He talked about how he was scheduled to leave the country on company business and because of the cost he could not afford treatment at this time. It was at this point that I identified myself to John as the company EAP representative. I assured him that his job would be protected and that our insurance covered all expenses but his deductible. With John's permission, I agreed to speak to his manager. John agreed and was admitted to treatment that night at 11:45 p. m.

That was seven years ago. John recently retired from his job and formed his own company. He remarried two years ago, and has reestablished a close relationship with his family. John has also sponsored several others into recovery, and served as a spokesperson for the benefits of recovery and the roles of EAPs.

The EAP may take a more active role in interventions as appropriate. On many occasions, we have conducted the intervention, although I find it best that when there is no reasonable company person available, the EAP can represent the company's policy and position.

SUMMARY

Workplace interventions can be the most successful way to address the progressive illness of alcoholism and drug addiction. Active employee assistance programs (EAPs) can be a vital resource to conduct or facilitate interventions. Referrals to the EAP may come from supervisors and unions, as well as family members.

Today, EAPs also see referrals as a result of court-ordered DWI evaluations, drug-free workplace policies, social service agencies, and many internal company departments including: Medical, Safety, and Human Resources. However, the EAP receives the referral; the goal of intervention is to assist in interrupting the addiction disease process and begin a recovery procedure that can avert continued personal losses and ultimately, death.

The Sheet Metal Worker's International Association and the Sheet Metal and Air Conditioning Contractors Association have listed five principles of effective workplace interventions:

- Stick to the facts about duty performance.
- Have all documents available; don't rely on memory.
- Explain all the consequences if performance expectations are not met.
- Be supportive, honest, and above all, firm.
- No one likes to suggest that a friend or a colleague has a problem.

The critical point to remember is that the supervisor is not helping the individual abuser or the business by neglecting the problem.

RESOURCES

For additional information on Workplace Intervention, contact the following organizations:

Employee Assistance Professional Association
2101 Wilson Blvd.
Arlington, VA 22201-3062
(703) 522-6272

National Clearinghouse for Alcohol & Drug Information
P.O. Box 2345
Rockville, MD 20852
(800) 729-6686
(301) 468-2600

Substance Abuse Information Database
  Washington, DC
  (800) 775-SAID

Johnson Institute
  7205 Ohms Lanes
  Minneapolis, MN 55439-2159
  (800) 231-5165

Chapter 5

Professional Assistance Committees

Penelope P. Ziegler

INTRODUCTION

An extensive variety of intervention approaches, ranging from peer intervention to formalized professional intervention committees, are available to extend help to professionals in fields such as medicine, law, finance, ministry, and engineering. This chapter overviews the development and availability of intervention models for impaired physicians.

Impairment of professionals by alcoholism and other drug dependencies has been recognized throughout recorded history. Stories such as that of Johns Hopkins surgeon Dr. William S. Halstead, who struggled with addiction to cocaine and morphine throughout his career, also illustrate the difficulty that professionals have had in recognizing and assisting their impaired colleagues. Since the earliest days of the recovery movement, recovering professionals have recognized a special obligation to "carry the message" to their peers who have active addictive disorders. Mutual help support groups such as International Doctors in Alcoholics Anonymous (IDAA), International Lawyers in Alcoholics Anonymous, Social Workers, Helping Social Workers, and many others have given structure and impetus to these efforts to assist fellow professionals into recovery.

In the late 1960s, professional organizations began to recognize an ethical responsibility to identify and assist members of the profession who were impaired. Beginning as a grassroots effort at the local and state level, the impairment issue became the focus of national professional organizations and associations. In 1973, the Council on Mental Health of the American Medical Association published an important paper titled "The Sick Physician," which stated unequivocally the ethical mandate incumbent on physicians to help their impaired colleagues to seek treatment or, alternatively, to cease practicing while impaired. Peer intervention was recognized as the most effective means of breaking the "conspiracy of silence" that often surrounds the addicted professional, enabling him or her to continue to deny, minimize, or rationalize chemical use.[1]

THE PEER INTERVENTION CONCEPT

Building on the concept of peer intervention, most state medical associations developed volunteer impairment committees whose function was to receive reports from concerned colleagues, attempt to verify this information, and arrange for intervention, confrontation, and referral to treatment for the affected physicians. Members of the committees were often physicians with a personal history of alcoholism and/or drug addiction who were in recovery[2] or psychiatrists or other physicians with special interest and/or expertise in addictive disorders.

The actual intervention often took place in the style of a "twelve-step call." This approach, perhaps the earliest form of peer intervention, was an outgrowth of Alcoholics Anonymous' twelfth step, ". . . we tried to carry this message to alcoholics." Reaching out to the suffering alcoholic by having the recovering person share his or her own experience, strength, and hope proved to be a powerful tool for helping an impaired colleague to accept treatment.

One approach to peer intervention popularized by G. Douglas Talbott and his associates in the Georgia Impaired Physician Program was a model in which a group of two or more recovering physicians visited the impaired physician, often several times, with the goal of convincing him or her to enter a treatment program. The intervening persons might share their own experiences during active addiction, describe the treatment experience and how it was helpful, share information about their current life situations, with emphasis on the great improvements which have resulted from entering recovery, and describe some of the negative consequences that could be expected to occur if the addictive disorder continues to progress unchecked. They may encourage the impaired physician to talk about the problems which she or he is experiencing now, and help to relate these to the use of alcohol and/or drugs. Often special attention is paid to the impact of the drinking/drug use on family relationships.[3]

This type of intervention departs from AA traditions in that the interventionists also describe in vivid detail the serious consequences to the individual's career and practice if he or she refuses to cooperate with the recommendations being made. Considerable pressure and coercion may be brought to bear to convince the impaired professional to enter treatment.

Other professional groups had similar early experiences with peer assistance. Nursing, dentistry, pharmacy, law, and various groups of clergy and religious formed peer assistance committees or similarly organized programs which maintained a central office and trained volunteers to be ready to respond when a colleague needed help.[4] Although very effective in helping many professionals to find treatment and recovery, these early programs were seriously limited by their volunteer nature and were unable to meet all the demands placed upon them.

The professional assistance movement was supported and encouraged in its growth by clinical research data which indicated positive outcomes and good prognoses for professionals who accepted treatment. Follow-up studies of professionals treated at centers such as Mayo Clinic,[5] Menninger Clinic,[6] Hazelden,[7] and Ridgeview[8] validated the usefulness of peer intervention and support. In her 1984 study, LeClair Bissell conducted sequential interviews with recovering physicians, dentists, nurses, attorneys, and social workers. Her study showed fairly low overall rates of relapse between interviews.[9]

During the 1980s, as the demand for professional assistance programs increased and the scope of the issues broadened, many state medical societies and other professional associations moved in the direction of developing professionally staffed assistance programs. These programs initially were called Impaired Physician Programs, Impaired Nurses Committee, etc. Later the names were modified to Physician Health Program, Lawyers Concerned for Lawyers, or other variations intended to destigmatize and convey a positive, rehabilitative posture. These programs hired addiction and mental health professionals as staff members. The Medical Society of New Jersey recruited a physician, Dr. David I. Canavan, as full-time medical director of its program[10]; many other states later followed this example. State Medical Society programs today are structured in a variety of models.

The Volunteer Intervention-Only Committee

This format is still in use by many states with a small physician population. Committee members participate in structured interventions whose goal is to convince the physician to enter treatment. The committee takes no responsibility for the outcome of treatment or for monitoring compliance on the part of the impaired professional.

Professionally Staffed Intervention and Monitoring Program

In this model, the medical society hires addiction and mental health professionals to run a multifaceted program which receives information about possible impaired physicians; verifies and obtains additional data; intervenes to encourage the physician to seek assessment and treatment at an approved facility; works with the treatment provider(s) to develop a plan of continued treatment and monitoring; collects data related to the participant's ongoing recovery status and activities; and based on these data, provides advocacy on behalf of compliant participants.

Medical Director Program

Many of the professionally staffed programs have a part-time or full-time medical director who is a physician with specialized training in addiction medicine and psychiatry. The medical director's role varies, but usually includes participation in interventions and in the ongoing monitoring process to assess participants' progress in treatment and recovery, as well as educational activities to increase awareness of the program in the medical community and to raise consciousness regarding the issue of professional impairment among practicing physicians, residents, medical students, hospital administrators, etc.

Contracted Program

In this model, the medical society contracts with an outside agency (usually a treatment provider) to provide interventional and monitoring services to impaired physicians who fall under the program's jurisdiction.

Licensing Board Diversion Program

In some states, the medical licensing board has developed a program for impaired physicians which allows the board to *divert from prosecution* licensees whom it finds to be suffering from an addictive or psychiatric disorder, referring them instead to a rehabilitative/ monitoring alternative. Such programs often function in ways similar to the medical society programs, but participation is limited to physicians who are known to the board and who meet the board's criteria for diversion. These programs may exist in parallel and cooperative with that state's medical society program. However, in some states with diversion programs, no comprehensive medical society program is offered.

Local and Institutional Programs

In addition to statewide programs, many health care organizations have localized committees or programs specifically designed to assist professionals practicing within that institution, group, etc. Hospital-based peer assistance committees usually work in cooperation with the state medical society program, receiving collegial concerns, exploring that work-related incidents which appear to be alcohol- or drug-related, and facilitating intervention and referral.[11] Some such committees are also involved in ongoing monitoring activities when a physician returns to practice. Some large medical centers have professionally staffed physician assistance programs which combine the functions of a peer assistance committee and an employee assistance program.[12] Nurses, pharmacists, physical therapists and other professionals employed by the hospital are usually served by the institution's employee assistance program.

Some county medical societies have physician assistance committees which work cooperatively with state society programs to facilitate identification, intervention, and ongoing monitoring. These groups also play a critical educational role within their medical communities, and in some cases have raised funds to help financially destitute physicians cover the cost of treatment.

The American Medical Association, which provided assistance and direction to state societies in developing peer assistance programs, has developed the Physicians' Health Foundation, which sponsors conferences and working group meetings to further knowledge and understanding of health problems which disrupt physicians' careers and personal lives.

Specialty societies have also contributed to the growing awareness and attention being paid to the issue of chemical dependency among physicians. For example, the American Society of Anesthesiology has launched an aggressive educational program for residents and their families aimed at raising consciousness about the special risks to practitioners of that specialty.[13]

Other professions today are also involved in efforts to assist their members to deal with and recover from addictive diseases. Dentists, nurses, social workers, psychologists, pharmacists, clergy and religious, veterinarians, attorneys, judges, anthropologists, and other professionals have developed local, state, and national support systems for members in need of assistance.[14]

A wide variety of intervention techniques are in use by various programs, and the actual mechanisms of intervention are continuing to evolve as changes in the health care delivery system impact on the process of peer assistance. Some approaches to intervention include those described in the following text.

Structured Peer Intervention

This is a carefully planned, rehearsed, and scripted approach in which fellow professionals with access to information about the professional's behavior meet with the individual to present their concerns, to encourage the individual to enter treatment, and to explore the possible consequences of refusal. As in a structured family intervention, efforts are made to focus on colleagues' concerns in a supportive, nonpunitive manner, and there is often one or more participants who are recovering themselves and can share some of their own experiences, offering reassurance and hope. Family members are sometimes included in this type of intervention, and can provide further powerful incentives to acceptance of treatment. If the professional assistance committee or program is involved, the professional can be offered confidentiality and advocacy by that program if he or she agrees to accept rehabilitation.

The peer intervention is a powerful tool for breaking down denial and initiating recovery. It is less commonly used today than in previous years for several reasons. The usual goal of a structured intervention is to convince the individual to enter an inpatient or residential treatment program. If the professional does not go immediately into a supportive, protected environment, there is concern that the overwhelming emotions aroused by the intervention process could lead to impulsive behavior and even to suicide, of which several cases are documented.

With the increasing difficulty of obtaining clearance from insurance carriers for inpatient treatment, and the requirement by some managed care systems that the patient fail outpatient treatment prior to being approved for inpatient care, there is increased anxiety about the possible dangers and liabilities of structured intervention. Fear of litigation has also contributed to the decreased use of this approach, although actual lawsuits have been extremely uncommon.

Case Example 1: George S.

A thirty-eight-year-old married male attorney, George S., practicing in a large corporate law firm, has had increasing difficulty controlling his alcohol use. Always a regular drinker, he has had several episodes of drunkenness at company functions and with clients. His productivity is decreasing, and two clients have complained about his sloppy appearance. Rumors about marital problems are the talk of the office.

The managing partner of the firm decides to contact the State Bar Association's confidential Lawyers Concerned for Lawyers program. Its director helps the reporting attorney to identify others in the firm who are willing to participate in the intervention and who have witnessed specific examples of George's loss of control. One of these colleagues, a young attorney whose wife is close to George's spouse, contacts George's wife; she is fearful at first, but also quite relieved that something is finally being done about his drinking.

The group of three colleagues and the wife meet together with the LCL director, and share their information and observations. The group learns that George's wife has been worried and angry for two years, and has already threatened to leave if he does not go for help. They review the data and develop a script for the intervention, as well as a plan for admission to a treatment facility. A decision is made to have the managing partner take the "hard line" on consequences of resistance to treatment, while the LCL director (himself a recovering alcoholic) and one of the younger partners will take the more supportive, compassionate roles.

The group meets one additional time to rehearse the script, and the appointment is made for the actual intervention, with George being told that the managing partner wants to meet with him to discuss some problems with a client. Despite some initial anger and suspiciousness, especially toward his wife, George ultimately accepts admission to the treatment center.

Administrative Intervention

Often following a consultation with the peer assistance committee or program, an individual with supervisory authority over the professional meets with him or her to present the data and concern, and to refer the professional for appropriate evaluation. For example, in the hospital setting, such an intervention may be performed by the department chairman, director of nursing, hospital administrator or Vice President of Medical Affairs. In most such cases, the professional will be placed on medical or administrative leave pending the outcome of the evaluation, and the appointment or initial contact with either the evaluator or the peer assistance program will be made prior to the conclusion of the interview.

Hospital medical staff bylaws and/or employee personnel policies may specify the procedure to be followed in investigating a possibly impaired professional and the consequences of his or her refusal to cooperate with the recommended assessment. If no such "Fit for Duty" and/or impairment policies exist, the state medical society's peer assistance program may be helpful to the hospital in formulating appropriate guidelines.

Case Example 2: Stan L.

A forty-five-year-old, divorced surgeon, Stan L., is suspected of diverting drugs from the intensive care unit narcotics cabinet. Several reports have been made by nurses indicating missing drugs when Stan is in the area; strange behavior including falling asleep in the on-call room and being difficult to arouse; leaving the operating room in the middle of a case; and remaining at the hospital all night when not on call. The department chairman discusses the case with the Vice President of Medical Affairs and together they contact the Physicians' Health Program (PHP) for consultation.

It is decided that the department chairman will meet with Stan as soon as possible, express concern over the behaviors which have been documented, and request an immediate observed urine specimen. Referral to the PHP will be offered as an alternative to disciplinary action and reporting, and the physician will be offered a medical leave of absence, provided he agrees to treatment.

The following day, the department chairman meets with Stan as planned. Although at first there is angry denial and refusal to provide the requested urine specimen, continued supportive insistence on the part of the chairman prevails. Stan breaks down and admits that he has been stealing and using the drugs. After a telephone conversation with the medical director of the PHP, he is immediately admitted to an inpatient detoxification unit to begin treatment.

Peer Assistance Program Intervention

When a referral is made to the peer assistance committee or program, the professional may be contacted by letter, telephone call, or personal visit from the medical director or other staff member. The modality utilized depends on the urgency of the situation, the nature of the data indicating impairment, and the available information predicting the professional's likely response. As in other approaches, the goal is to accomplish a referral for assessment and, if indicated, treatment.

Case Example 3: Bob J.

The wife of a twenty-seven-year-old pharmacist, Bob J., contacts the Pharmacists Aiding Pharmacists (PAP) hotline with concerns about her husband's use of opiate and sedative pills. She has confronted him several times, and he keeps promising to stop. Last night she found three empty pill bottles under the mattress. She is angry and frightened, but states that she still loves him and wants to help him if possible. She also reports that at least two of his co-workers are aware that he has been taking pills.

At the request of the PAP staff member, these other pharmacists call the PAP and give specific information about their observations. The director of the PAP calls Bob on the phone at home on his day off, and makes an appointment to see him in two hours. After a discussion of the data, the concerns of his wife and colleagues, and the consequences of refusal, Bob agrees to undergo assessment and schedules an appointment with an evaluator approved by the PAP for the following day. Following the assessment, he enters an intensive outpatient program, while taking a medical leave of absence from work.

Family Intervention

Most peer assistance programs do not facilitate family interventions, but will refer a concerned family member to an interventionist who is experienced in working with professional families. A representative from the peer assistance program may participate in the intervention if this is appropriate. Family interventions are especially useful in cases where there is evidence of progressive chemical dependency but no clear indication of professional impairment. In the earlier stages of addiction, the professional may be experiencing significant family and relationship problems, but has retained sufficient control to prevent job-related problems or incidents.

The success of any intervention depends on having sufficient leverage to either break through the affected individual's denial system or, failing that, to convince that professional to enter treatment despite ongoing denial in order to protect his or her professional and/or personal standing (license, job, marriage, etc.) A variety of techniques can be utilized in preparing for the intervention which can maximize the chances for success in convincing the individual to accept treatment.

A successful intervention depends on having sufficient facts with which to confront the reluctant professional, facts which have convinced the intervening group that there are enough data to support the conclusion that a substance use disorder is likely to be present and require treatment. Using a medical rather than a legal model, the question being asked in data collection is: "What are the signs and symptoms which indicate that there is something wrong, and that the "something" may involve chemical use?" In many cases, there may have been a precipitating event which clearly indicates that the professional has lost control of his or her chemical use. However, more often the situation involves a series of incidents which are suggestive of a problem, but do not offer sufficient data to draw a certain conclusion.

Collecting data regarding a professional can usually be organized broadly to examine several areas of functioning likely to yield useful information.

Professional Function

Has there been a change in the person's ability to function in his or her profession, or other indicators in the workplace that the person is experiencing difficulty? Some specific areas of inquiry which may turn up important data include the following:

1. *Review of charts or records* for legibility, coherence, completeness, and specific indicators of drug use (in medical setting) such as discrepancies in medication records (nurses), excessive medication orders (physicians), excessive stock orders (pharmacists).
2. *Review of professional and legal records* for absenteeism (especially before or after weekends off, vacations, holidays); reprimands or suspensions for inappropriate conduct, alcohol on the breath, missed appointments or deadlines, and/or excessive absenteeism; arrests for DWI, DUI, drunk and disorderly, or possession of illegal substances.
3. For a hospital employee or physician on the hospital staff, *a review of the hospital pharmacy records* can be very useful. Many addicted nurses and hospital pharmacists fill prescrip-

tions for themselves or family members at the hospital pharmacy which have been forged or have been obtained from unsuspecting hospital physicians. A physician may write multiple prescriptions for self-use or for family members. In some areas, it is possible to obtain a record of the physician's prescriptions at all area pharmacies allowing detection of a pattern of prescribing for self-use in the name of family members, fraudulent or unsuspecting patients, etc. Information about the availability of such a computer search can be obtained from a local pharmacist, from the state bureau of narcotics control, or from the appropriate peer assistance program.

4. *Review of behavior*—A change in the professional's usual style of interacting with others may be a useful indicator of problems. This is particularly true if there is a pattern of unusual reactions or the person seems to have had a dramatic change in personality from his or her previous pattern. In many cases, significant persons in the professional's work setting, such as office staff, colleagues, co-workers, supervisors, and even patients or clients may be aware that there is something wrong, but either do not know what to do about it or are afraid of causing the person harm. When a hospital, professional firm, or other professional work setting has been able to create an environment in which professionals can trust that efforts will be made to help, not discipline, the impaired professional, it is often possible to encourage concerned peers to provide meaningful data about these behavioral changes. However, in many environments, the level of fear is too high, and just interviewing others about the possibility that a peer has a problem creates an atmosphere of paranoia and anger which can undermine the efforts to prepare for an intervention.

There are many resources available to professionals affected by chemical dependency. The national or state professional association for the profession in question can most likely provide up-to-date information about that profession's position on the question of impairment, and can direct concerned persons to the appropriate resources for assistance.

REFERENCES

1. AMA Council on Mental Health. (1973). "The sick physician." *JAMA* *223:* 684-867.

2. Crosby, L.R. and Bissell, L. (1989). *To care enough.* Minneapolis: Johnson Institute Books, pp. 55-68.

3. Talbott, G. Douglas. (1984). "Elements of the impaired physician program." *J Med Assoc GA 73:* 749-751.

4. Bissell, L. and Haberman, P (1984). *Alcoholism in the professions.* New York: Oxford University Press, pp. 138-170.

5. Morse, R.M. (1984). "Prognosis of physicians treated for alcoholism and drug dependence." *JAMA 251:* 743-746.

6. Johnson, R.P. and Connelly, J.C. (1981). "Addicted physicians: A closer look." *JAMA 245:* 253-257.

7. Kliner, D.J. (1980). "Treatment outcome of alcoholic physicians." *Journal of Studies on Alcohol 41:* 1217-1220.

8. Talbott, G.D., Gallegos, K.V., Wilson, PO. and Porter, T.L. (1981). "The Medical Association of Georgia's Disabled Doctors Program: A five-year review." *J Med Assoc GA 70:* 545-559.

9. Bissell and Haberman, pp. 96-118.

10. Reading, E.G. (1992). "Nine years' experience with chemically dependent physicians— The New Jersey experience." *MD Med J 41:* 325-329.

11. Samkoff, J.S. and McDermott, R.W. (1990). "Structure of a hospital's impaired physician committee." *PA Med:* 34-39.

12. White, R.K., McDuff, D. and Schwartz, R. (1992). "Hospital-based professional assistance committees: Literature review and guidelines." *MD Med J 41:* 305-309.

13. Arnold, W.P. (1993). "Survey of substance abuse in anesthesiology Training programs." *ASA Newsletter 57:* 21-22.

14. Crosby and Bissell, pp. 273-280.

Chapter 6

Adolescent Intervention Strategies

James Crowley

Early intervention is a concept easily understood in the context of a progressive and chronic disease such as alcoholism. Yet, any action that is "early" is early only in relation to an event or a condition that might have happened to a person had the action not been taken. When early intervention is used to help an adolescent who is becoming involved with alcohol/other drugs, we may never be certain what is actually being prevented.

When we first encounter young people, some are already addicted to alcohol and/or other drugs, and it is clear where their progressive and chronic disease will lead. There are also those young people who, without some type of intervention, will become more and more involved with alcohol and/or other drugs and eventually become addicted. But most young people who become involved with alcohol and/or other drugs, rather than developing chronic addictions, will suffer other harmful consequences. These could be stunted emotional, psychological, social, and/or intellectual growth; lost opportunities that will affect the quality of their lives; or injury or death in an alcohol and/or other drug-related accident.

Whereas adult intervention focuses primarily on the addicted person and the problems related to his or her addiction, early intervention programs for adolescents cannot focus exclusively on the addicted persons or simply on the harmful consequences of their behavior. With adolescents, alcohol and/or other drug use *alone* can be a legitimate criterion for intervention. Problems related to drug use may be one criterion, along with frequency of use, quantity of drugs used and other factors, by which to determine the type of intervention called for, but we cannot assume that nonproblem drug use by adolescents is acceptable.

Most people would not approve of a thirteen-year-old girl drinking a couple of beers three times a week, even if she does not have a behavior problem at home and is doing well in school. Likewise, approval would not be there for the football star who gets stoned each night, but continues to do well academically. For families, professionals, schools, and communities, the only reasonable and responsible position is that no alcohol and/or other drug use by children or adolescents is acceptable.

Some parents, educators, and professionals will argue that the adolescent's alcohol or other drug use is simply experimentation, and therefore a harmless stage of normal development, a rite of passage. Others view alcohol and other drug use as purely symptomatic of some other underlying problem; when the real problem is addressed, the need to use alcohol and/or other drugs will be eliminated. If no alcohol or other drug use by adolescents is acceptable, intervention into any use becomes a priority, whether that use is a primary or secondary problem. Abstinence does not necessarily simplify or alleviate all of the adolescent's difficulties, but psychotherapy to offer additional help cannot successfully proceed until the alcohol and other drug use ceases. Incremental intervention is a way to intervene with adolescents in a manner appropriate to their needs.

The structured intervention format used with family members confronting an alcoholic adult, which is designed to urge the person to accept treatment, is too much too soon for most adolescents. When interventions are done incrementally, beginning with the least disruptive, time-consuming, and expensive steps, many adolescents are able to make the necessary changes and avoid the more extensive steps that could involve long absences from home and school.

It is important to make some distinctions among the wide realm of adolescent drug-use problems that require a range of interventions. A low-level intervention may be effective with a person who merely uses alcohol and/or other drugs occasionally, whereas a high-level intervention is usually necessary for success with a person who is psychologically and physically dependent on these substances. For instance, while many young people can benefit from an intensive treatment program, there are those who do not need that service. Similarly, young people who can benefit from immediate and forceful disciplinary actions stand in contrast to those for whom discipline makes no difference at all.

Estimation of the severity of the adolescent's use often proves difficult until the user attempts to stop using. It is important to give the adolescent an opportunity to work on staying alcohol/other-drug-free in a low-level intervention environment and avoid the considerable disruption caused by another, possibly unnecessary, format. Even if the adolescent cannot stay drug-free, the behavior exhibited during this time provides useful data as to what additional steps are necessary.

Although effective early intervention programs can be established in or with the help of many systems, (e.g., criminal justice, religious, service agencies), a school-based early intervention program provides the greatest leverage for intervening into problems adversely affecting young people. School is where young people are, and the school has contact with almost every young person in the community. School is also the place where a trained staff educates and nurtures young people, monitoring their growth through their adolescent years. Clearly, if we want to reach as many young people as possible, school is *the* place to do it early and in a more efficient and effective manner. For these reasons, this chapter will focus on early incremental intervention programs in schools, with the understanding that parents and other systems need to and should be actively involved.

INCREMENTAL INTERVENTION

The steps of an incremental early intervention program are: identification—recognizing cues or signs of problems; initial action—reacting appropriately to behavior problems; preassessment—determining what action steps need to be taken; referral—where to send adolescents for services which meet their needs; and support—offering assistance to young persons trying to make behavioral changes.

Identification is a process whereby cues or outright signs suggesting that something is wrong for the young person or that a problem is bothering him or her is recognized by those having influence or control over the young person. Anyone can identify these cues or signs—teachers, counselors, coaches, nurses, social workers, youth workers, clergy, parents, police/probation officers, or peers. The cues or signs may center around general behavior, academic performance, alcohol or other drug problems, or any other concern expressed by someone. Examples are include the following:

- A young person becomes increasingly belligerent at home and school.
- A student's academic performance becomes erratic or declines.
- A young person changes friends from nonusing adolescents to known drug users.
- A student is caught with some drug paraphernalia at school.

In order to increase the rate of identification of drug-using young people, the various identifiers need to be educated on behavioral expectations for young people; what to look for—signs of symptoms of problems or family issues; what not to do—enabling behaviors; what to do—positive action steps; and who can help—available referral resources.

Initial action is being able to react appropriately to problem behaviors. It is crucial to early intervention. When a young person is facing a serious problem, there are a variety of ways initial action can begin. The student may ask for help. A teacher, parent, or other professional may express concern about certain behavior(s) to the young person. One concerned person may consult with another regarding the problem behaviors. A counselor may call a parent to discuss what is being observed. A referral may be made to an early intervention specialist or student assistance professional. Initial action can be taken by any person who is concerned about the behaviors they have identified.

When a student is identified because of a rule violation such as intoxication or possession of drug paraphernalia, the actions to be taken are usually specified in the school disciplinary code or laws of the community. Procedures are not so specific, however, when poor performance or negative changes in behavior are noted or when there is simply an intuitive feeling that something is going on with the young person. In these cases, as a first step, it is best if the concerned person talks with the adolescent and possibly the parents. If the identifier wants only to make a referral to an early intervention specialist or the student assistance team, it is best if those receiving the referral talk with the student and/or parents before taking further action.

Once the student body has been educated about the early intervention process and the student assistance program has had some success allowing trust to be developed, troubled students will also be identified by their peers. Young people who have experienced their own successful intervention and who clearly understand that the help they received is what their sibling or friend desperately needs will be especially inclined to identify troubled peers.

Initial action steps which correspond to very low-level interventions are talking with a student about the concerns and clarifying the behavioral expectations. It is possible that a young person may not realize that the behavior is out of line, and once that is made clear, he or she can alter the behavior. Providing young people with realistic information about the dangers of alcohol and other drug use may also help some to decide to abstain. It may be helpful to contract with the young person to change his or her behavior for a period of time; for example, to stop using alcohol and/or other drugs for a month or two to see if he or she can be abstinent. Sometimes working together with the parents brings additional assistance and support for behavior change. Many young people will not engage in negative behavior when their parents make it specifically clear that the behavior is unacceptable and will follow through with consequences if necessary.

If these low-level interventions succeed in the required behavior changes, the success shows no need for further action. If not, the lack of success is additional data that a higher level of intervention is necessary and that a referral to an early intervention specialist is appropriate.

There are several reasons why concerned individuals will hesitate to take any initial action. They might believe that the young person is a "lost cause" and not worth the effort, or that the behavior is not serious enough: "He's only drinking beer." Some refuse to be the "bad guy," and think it borders on being a narc. There are some who believe they *alone* can solve this young person's problems, and so refuse to involve others. Sometimes a concerned person believes that it is a family issue and therefore none of his or her business, or that getting involved is not a requirement of his or her position. A few may not trust the early intervention process; therefore, it is important to educate potential identifiers about the process and to help them build trust in the process and their referral sources.

Preassessment, or preliminary assessment, is the next step in incremental intervention. The term "preassessment" is used to distinguish this process from diagnostic evaluations done by treatment centers, mental health agencies, or specific alcohol, and other drug-assessment services. The goal of preassessment is to gather the information needed to make a decision about what should be done next. The whole point of incremental intervention is to methodically walk young people through successive levels of intervention. If we can identify those who use alcohol and/or other drugs, but who do not have critical problems, and engage them in low-level intervention, we can reserve the more intense, often limited services for those who appear to have more serious problems.

Any system can provide this component; however, the school student assistance program is an ideal resource. Once a referral has been made, those receiving the referral can verify that the concerned person has already talked to the young person to clarify the problem, and that the young person is aware of what changes in behavior are expected. There are many ways to gather data, and the most effective student assistance programs do not rely on any single method.

Data-gathering forms designed to assess the young person's attitudes, general behavior, and academic performance can be sent to all adults in the system who interact with the young person. School records are also a good source of information on past behavior, such as grades, extracurricular participation, disciplinary problems, and attendance. Concrete information from parents can help fill out the picture of their child's behavior, especially at home and with friends.

Sometimes an interview with the young person can be an important source of information. It can also be used just to make the young person aware of the situation and to check his or her general attitude about the problem issues. An interview is an opportunity to offer personal support and learn the young person's viewpoint, level of concern about, and control of their behavior. New data and general impressions may also be gained.

Another service is a group approach to preassessment. A group setting can facilitate attempts to help young people increase their knowledge and awareness about how their lives are being affected by alcohol and/or other drug use. Group members can share their observations and also use peer confrontation to break through some of the barriers some young people use to stop themselves from seeing what is really happening.

Because parent involvement and cooperation is necessary to effectively intervene with a young person who uses alcohol and/or other drugs, intervention counselors and educators need to support both the parents and their children when intervening. Parents must be involved because of their right to know when their child has violated the law and/or has a significant health problem. They can contribute greatly to the assessment/intervention process because they have data to add to that of the school. Their reactions can also give an indication of their concern, interest, and ability to help the young person. Some parents might need to be reminded of their responsibilities in regard to controlling and helping to change their child's negative behavior. All parents must be made aware of what actions the school or law enforcement can take, given parent's cooperation or noncooperation.

The three main criteria for performance referrals in early identification programs are an increase in absences, a decline in grades, and an increase in disciplinary problems. How and when the parents should be brought into the intervention process is not always clear. If there has been a violation of law or school regulations, of course, parents are contacted immediately. If it is a performance referral, it may be advantageous to wait until clear data has been collected by the school and can be presented to the parents. Some intervention counselors prefer to personally notify the parents, sometimes calling the parents while the young person is present. Another technique is to urge the young person to tell his or her parent(s) and then have the parent(s) call the counselor. In all cases, at least one of the parents should be eventually contacted and met with, sooner rather than later. It is important for the intervention counselor to avoid the trap of "keeping secrets" for the adolescent. It should be clearly explained to the young person that the boundaries for confidentiality include his or her parents. Parental cooperation must also be enlisted to ensure that the young person follows through on suggestions for assistance.

It requires patience for adults to work with young people during the early stages of intervention. Assessment of adolescent alcohol and other drug problems is rarely a cut-and-dry process. Rather, it often entails monitoring the young person for a time to see what patterns emerge. This ability to monitor ongoing behavior differentiates early intervention programs from outside assessment services in the community. An ongoing monitoring process is frequently used in schools when a young person appears to have some problems with alcohol and/or other drugs or other issues, but the picture is not yet clear enough for definite action. Schools are in the best position to monitor very closely how well particular young people are behaving.

Just as a variety of means can be used to gather data, more than one person can assess the available data. Early intervention specialists or the student assistance team can consider such questions as: What are all the areas of trouble for this student? Is any one problem area emerging as the main focus of concern? Are the data complete? Should more information be sought? Are the data consistent? With the goal of preassessment being to decide what, if any, action to take, members of the student assistance team can make appropriate decisions by reviewing a young person's needs in light of available school services or services outside the school.

A *referral* may be made to an in-school educational program or support group after making a preliminary assessment. Obviously, an in-school referral is going to be less intrusive and disruptive to the life of the young person, and can yield tremendous benefits. In some rare cases, this may be the only referral option because community services are lacking or nonexistent. When the referral is that the parents take the young person to an outside service for formal assessment, family counseling, or treatment, the outside agency will need the background information gathered by the early intervention program. The parents will probably also need support to take this action step. One way to offer support is to provide parents with information packets that describe local resources and how to contact them.

Once a referral is made, the early intervention staff should follow it up to see if the young person or the family made the contact and if the service suggested was appropriate. For the early intervention process to work successfully, schools, courts, and social service agencies should establish procedures that allow them to share confidential information in a manner consistent with the client's needs and rights. Agreements for releases of confidential information should be drawn up to meet school, state, and federal regulations.

In adult intervention, the process usually is complete with the referral. With adolescents, however, the additional component of support is necessary.

Support is important because change does not come easily. When people begin to make changes in their lives, they frequently need encouragement. Adults recovering from addiction can usually avoid their past-using friends and places, but that is harder for recovering adolescents. Young people who are attempting to stay drug-free are usually in the same school where they previously used and in class with former-using buddies. Therefore, if young people are to refrain from using alcohol and/or other drugs, with or without treatment, they need the support and help of their families, friends, peers, school staff, and any other person concerned about them. Aftercare therapy from a treatment center or service agency, support groups in schools and other systems, and attendance at Alcoholics Anonymous meetings are three primary ways to help young people maintain their abstinence. It is also important to remember that alcohol and other drug users are not the only young people who need ongoing support. Youth in crisis related to family dysfunction or other issues also need ongoing support.

SUMMARY

The principles of intervention are the same for adolescents as adults—concerned persons share specific information to help the adolescent or adult see the harmful consequences of his or her behavior. The intervention structure or format differs. For adults, the behavior is usually addiction to alcohol and/or other drugs with the goal being acceptance of treatment. The actual event takes place at a particular place and time, and involves primarily family members. For adolescents, the behavior is *any* use of alcohol and other drugs, or any behavior that may lead to usage. Adolescent intervention occurs in increments of meetings, interviews, and/or conferences, during which information from a wide variety of sources, including school staff, peers, and family members is shared. The incremental intervention format is an effective way to intervene with young persons in a manner appropriate to their needs. The primary goal of incremental intervention is to methodically walk young people through successive levels of intervention. Low-level interventions are used with those who do not have critical problems, reserving the more intense services for those who appear to have more serious problems.

Although effective early intervention programs can be established in or with the help of many systems, a school-based program provides the greatest leverage in intervening into problems affecting young people. Each program identifies the signs of a problem and takes initial action to respond appropriately. A preassessment determines what action steps are necessary, after which the young person is referred to services which meet his or her needs. Support is offered to those trying to make positive behavior changes.

Parental involvement and cooperation is necessary to effectively intervene with the young person. Intervention specialists need to support both the parents and their children when intervening for problems. Young people trying to refrain from using alcohol and/or other drugs, with or without treatment, need the support and help of their families, friends, peers, and school staff.

CASE EXAMPLES

Case Example 1: Greg

Identification

Greg is sixteen-years old and a junior in high school. He was found intoxicated in the school parking lot by the health teacher.

Initial Action

Greg's parents were called to pick him up; and in compliance with school policy, he was suspended for three days. The assistant principal then turned the issue over to the student assistance team. The team requested academic and behavior reports from all of Greg's teachers.

Preassessment

Greg's teachers, in general, reported inconsistent attendance, a drop in grades, and a belligerent attitude in class. School discipline records showed that this was Greg's second alcohol violation on school property. In a meeting with Greg's parents, the student assistance counselor discovered that Greg had become a major discipline problem, had threatened both of his parents, and was hanging around with a group of neighborhood "druggies." In an interview with Greg, he displayed a very defensive posture and accused his parents and the school of harassing him. He said he drank occasionally and had for three years, but no more than other guys his age. He did not see his drinking as the problem everyone else was making it out to be.

Referral

Based on the information obtained, the student assistance team suggested that the parents obtain a formal assessment of Greg's alcohol use. The assessment determined that Greg was in need of in-patient treatment, which he is now completing.

Support

A member of the student assistance team visits Greg while he is in treatment, arranged for tutoring, and is taking part in the aftercare planning with the treatment counselor. Greg will participate in an abstinent support group in school when he returns and will continue attendance at Alcoholics Anonymous in the community.

Case Example 2: Mary

Identification

Mary is fifteen years old and in tenth grade. She seemed to be withdrawing from active participation in class, and her grades, which were normally a B average, dropped to C. She also seemed preoccupied and often very sad.

Initial Action

Mary's social studies teacher became quite concerned. She talked with Mary's homeroom teacher, who also expressed concern and in addition said that Mary's attendance was becoming sporadic. The social studies teacher expressed her concerns to Mary. When Mary explained that she was having problems at home, the teacher suggested Mary see a student assistance counselor. An appointment was made for her.

Preassessment

In an interview with Mary, the student assistance counselor learned that Mary's father had been drinking heavily during the past year, and was very abusive to the family each night when he came home drunk. Mary had not been able to do her schoolwork, and was worried about her mother and two younger sisters. Mary said she went to parties a couple of times a month and did smoke marijuana just to relax and reduce her stress. Her mother was interviewed by the counselor. The mother was also concerned about Mary's stress and schoolwork, but felt overwhelmed and said she had her hands full with her husband.

Referral

With her mother's consent and support, Mary agreed to join a "Children of Alcoholics" support group at her school. She further consented to sign an agreement not to use alcohol or other drugs for six months as a requirement to be in the group. The counselor also gave the mother a list of Al-Anon meetings and a list of family counseling and intervention services.

Support

Mary is in the support group at school and is also receiving academic support through the school guidance office.

Case Example 3: Kristen and Billy

Identification

Kristen sought out the student assistance counselor to discuss her concerns about her boyfriend's drinking. She had heard a talk in health class which described the stages of drinking and drug usage and it raised her concern. Billy, a seventeen-year-old in twelfth grade, drank heavily and used drugs every weekend. Kristen said it was hurtful to their relationship.

Initial Action

The student assistance counselor asked Kristen to detail Billy's use, his behavior related to that use, and her concerns and feelings about it. After reviewing this information, the counselor requested that Kristen ask Billy to come in and see him. The counselor and Kristen role-played the proposed conversation with Billy until Kristen was comfortable in asking. Billy reluctantly agreed to see the counselor, but only to prove that Kristen had blown things out of proportion.

Preassessment

Billy was defensive about his use. He claimed that he only had "a couple of beers" on weekends, a lot less than the other seniors. He further claimed that Kristen was becoming a prude and that he was tired of her nagging him. The student assistance counselor reported the data shared by Kristen. Billy was somewhat stunned, but said Kristen was making a mountain out of a mole hill. The counselor expressed his concern to Billy, and said he thought Billy was deluded about his use and minimizing the impact it was having on him and Kristen. The counselor said he planned to check with Billy's teachers to see if they had any concerns and suggested that Billy talk to his parents about this conversation. Billy was unwilling to do that, but said that the counselor could call his parents. Billy thought that his parents would say he was doing well. He did not think his dad would care if he had a couple of beers once in a while, especially if Kristen drove the car. The behavior report forms from the staff did not indicate any clear problems. The football coach was concerned that Billy had suddenly quit football. Billy said it was because the coach was a jerk. Kristen said it was because football interfered with his time for drinking with buddies. The counselor contacted the parents and met with them. They were unaware of Billy's drinking, and were very concerned.

Referral

It was decided that Billy would attend an assessment group in school. This would allow all those concerned, including Billy, to get a better understanding of the extent of his alcohol and other drug use. Billy also agreed to stop using, which he claimed was "no big deal." The parents and Billy agreed to obtain a formal assessment from an alcohol specialist if Billy broke his abstinence agreement. They also consented to follow the recommendation that would come at the end of the school assessment group.

Support

If Billy has a difficult time maintaining his sobriety following support group, he can join the abstinence support group at school and attend Alcoholic Anonymous in the community. If he quits using and seems to be doing well, he can simply be monitored and occasionally visit with the student assistance counselor.

Chapter 7

Intervention as Brief Family Therapy

Stuart A. Tiegel

The most difficult habit to break is
breaking the habit of others.

—Edwin W. Friedman
Friedman's Fables

INTRODUCTION

Some time ago, there was a series of "lightbulb" jokes popular at the office, hairdressers', therapist conferences, and the like. These jokes were rather benign and poked fun at all therapists. The core element, the punch line, satirized the apparent ineffectiveness of the therapeutic process. As this seems relevant to chemical dependence treatment and treatment motivation, let me give you an example of a "lightbulb" joke:

Question: How many therapists does it take to screw in a lightbulb?

Answer: Only one, but the lightbulb has to really want it!

We have been immersed in thinking that "if they really want it" is the only option when it comes to treatment for chemically dependent family members. Families that seek treatment for a chemically dependent member often feel sucked into a pit of despair. During this immobilizing time, traditional therapeutic solutions may become problems in themselves, delaying needed recovery. When families are in this pit of despair, it becomes essential to find tools other than shovels, which only cause families to go deeper and deeper into their abyss. Such tools can be simple to apply, and work incrementally without ever tackling more than is possible at any given time.

This chapter is about such a tool, another approach to treatment, based on an integration of Vernon Johnson's Intervention Model (JIM), Task Centered Clinical Social Work (TCSW), and Structural Systems Engagement (SSE). These three components comprise a focused, structured approach to a social work intervention for helping families *with or without the compliance of the identified patient.*

The focused family intervention (FFI) is an additional resource to treat intractable chemically dependent patients. It does not require that the identified patient ask for help. In this chapter, I will illustrate how this approach utilizes the strength, wisdom, and resources in the family to bring about change and promote the initiating and engaging steps in the recovery process. There is a primary goal for intervening with a family: simply stated, you must create change that is significant, observable, and acceptable. We often do not think of bottom lines in treatment; however, with a progressive, terminal illness, such as chemical dependence, we must. The focused family intervention helps us zero in on the bottom line, activating early recovery and planning for continued recovery.

Although intervention is a term associated with Vernon Johnson's innovative work in Minnesota, clinical social workers and family therapists have used similar approaches with a focused orientation in their practices with difficult problems including chemical dependence. This chapter will review selected intervention models and use illustrative cases to discuss the ways those models have been used effectively. The central themes in this chapter involve focused, active, compassionate, effective approaches to invite and formulate change with chemically dependent families.

SELECTED ACTIVE-ORIENTED INTERVENTION MODEL

Johnson's Intervention Model

Dr. Johnson describes intervention as follows:

A process by which harmful, progressive, and destructive effects of chemical dependency are interrupted and the chemically dependent person is helped to stop using mood-altering chemicals and to develop healthier ways of coping with his or her need and problems. It implies that the person need not be an emotional or physical wreck (or hit bottom) before such help can be given.[1]

Rarely do chemically dependent people arrive in a clinician's office requesting help. If they show up at all, it is to alter the consequences of their actions, not to face the real problem—their dependency on alcohol or other drugs. The intervention is a breakthrough because it shifts responsibility for creating change from the identified patient to the concerned, involved family members, and others significant in the life of the patient. It requires the assembling of this group, with a skilled clinician, to say: "We will help you live; we will not help you die." There is a paradigm shift from the passive to the active, the impotent to the empowered, with respect to the practices of the family. A declaration is made: "We will no longer be part of the problem; we will be part of the solution."

How does that happen? Although the details of Johnson's model have been reviewed in his book, the five-step model can be briefly summarized as follows:

1. Gather the intervention team
2. Gather the data
3. Rehearse
4. Establish logistics of meeting
5. Decide whether a professional should be used

I view this model as a basic outline inviting improvisation. A professional is recommended. He or she helps organize the intervention, sets up treatment reservations, provides a meeting place, and becomes an emotional traffic cop. Families often have extreme difficulty with data gathering in Step 2 as it requires honest, open discussion. This may be a unique experience for some families. It also requires agreeing on the "diagnosis" of a life threatening illness in a family member in absentia! The clinician helps to confirm the "diagnosis" by conveying that they must assume "If it walks like a duck, smells like a duck, and looks and quacks like a duck—it is a duck." Families can be experts at diagnosing their members effectively. A skilled interventionist can share Johnson's list of questions that help specify addictive patterns.[2]

Task-Focused Clinical Social Work Intervention and Families

Because clinical social workers provide approximately 65 percent of all mental health and substance abuse treatment nationally, they are in a position to act as interventionists. The clinical social workers' door is a portal of entry for many families.[3]

A basic historical clinical social work assumption is that the relational context is fundamental. "That man and his fellow creatures are seen as inseparable from their environment" suggests an interactive theme useful in thinking about the web of enabling and denial often evident in chemically dependent families.[4] However, relational context can cause confusion by not differentiating the concept of "coresponsibility" where all parties in a social system contribute to a shared reality.[5] This idea is much easier to understand as a concept than it is to apply.

Clinical social work embraces the view that active empowerment of families by reviving internal resources, searching for new ones, and doing things differently with existing resources promotes change. The goal of interventions is to have the family do something different by stopping the enabling and resolving the denial. This is best accomplished with the help of a clinician who can proceed with credibility, authority, and empathy—respecting the culture of the specific family. Also, the goal of any intervention must be to reach the desired outcome with a sense of time sensitivity and focus. In task-centered clinical social work,[6] there is much we can apply in intervening with chemically dependent families. As Reid says:

> Contextual change is important but target problems are the first priority. A fundamental principal of the task-centered approach is to concentrate on alleviating target problems through relatively simple, straightforward tasks. Any contextual change that occurs is an incidental, added benefit. Moreover, structural dysfunctions, underlying pathologies, and the like are left alone unless they intrude as obstacles.[7]

This gives us a road map. Change occurs through tasks. Good clinical tasks capture a problem sequence that invites a solution. Specifically, the task brings the problem into the present so it can be resolved in the present.

What is it we do when we invite families to intervene? We request that they stay focused on the targeted problem of chemical dependence, construct alternative scripts that describe their experience with the actively drug and/or alcohol using family member, rehearse, and act. (The case presentations will illustrate what occurs pre- and postintervention.)

In the task-centered approach there are a number of guiding principles:

1. Maintain a problem focus
2. Understand the context
3. Emphasize problem resolution and action
4. Establish a collaborative relationship between family and clinician
5. Maintain time sensitivity

Those who have conducted interventions know these principles well and appreciate the descriptive simplicity and complexity during implementation.

Let me refer to the caveats in summarizing the task-centered model as it is applied to the problem of chemical dependence. In most chemically dependent families, we face human beings having experienced repetitive problem sequences involving illness, crime, violence, destruction of family rituals, and often all hope that is an integral part of a family vision. In a task-centered approach, self-determined action replaces indecisiveness and wishful thinking.

STRUCTURAL SYSTEMS ENGAGEMENT (SSE) AND FAMILIES

The work done by Szapocznik and associates in the area of family therapy is an important development with respect to engaging chemically dependent families into treatment.[8] In focusing on the issue of active engagement in treatment for chemical dependency, it is an effective way to propel the intervention from conception to application.

SSE represents an integration that includes Minuchin's Structural Family Therapy[9] and Haley's Strategic Family Therapy approaches.[10] Although it is not the purpose of this chapter to review the extensive literature behind both these schools of therapy, a brief description of SSE would be helpful as an orientation. The three components characterizing this treatment orientation are as follows:

1. *System*—A view of the family as interactive, coresponsible, and interdependent.
2. *Structure*—Refers to repetitive, normative patterns, both functional and dysfunctional.
3. *Strategic*—Refers to the "how" of treatment as a highly focused way of intervening with simplicity and clinician responsibility for change.

The uniqueness of Szapoczik's work is relevant to chemical dependency treatment in that engagement into treatment is the major focus. On the one hand, the proactive family therapist talks of "the battle for structure" as the first phase of family therapy; on the other, SSE creates a context in which treatment appears irresistible. The therapist's presentation of countervailing propositions sets up within the family a selection of options, all of which will produce change. Tasks are employed to engage families in treatment, and a therapeutic double bind develops. The therapeutic double bind suggests to the family that treatment is inevitable, and that it is a more favorable option to maintaining the status. The fundamental purpose of the task or directives is to mobilize the strength in the family in order to do something very different. The clinician plays an extremely important role in SSE by offering options that are consistent with the family's wishes and its culture. Although the therapist is time sensitive in SSE, there is a patient nurturing of family interest in dealing with the pain of chemical dependence and reinforcing the desire to alter that pain and suffering.

CLINICAL EXAMPLES

In reviewing clinical material to illustrate Interventions, two have been selected that have a number of issues in common. In the first case, addiction was present for more than fifteen years, and considered chronic. In the second case, health concerns and motivation for treatment were major factors in the outcome.

Case Example 1: The Best Family

Background Information

Matt (not his real name) is a thhirty-two-year-old man living at home with his mother, father, and twenth-four-year-old brother. He had only brief periods of independent living as an adult. He has always maintained employment in his family's moderately successful business. His skills centered on inventory and purchasing. Matt called after being referred by his family physician who was concerned about his deteriorating health, possible liver damage, and a fifteen-year history of sedative/hypnotic (Quaaludes) dependence, requiring two psychiatric hospitalizations, frequent emergency room visits for treatment of accidental injuries, two DUIs, loss of driver's license, and three attempts at outpatient psychiatric treatment (in individual psychotherapy).

Assessment

Matt was in denial about his fifteen-year continuous dependency on Quaaludes. He felt that recreational pharmacology suited him, and that he was in control. There seemed to be family pressure to engage in treatment that would have a better outcome and involve them. Of course, Matt wanted individual treatment without family involvement. The therapist stated that with his continued family loyalty and the discrepancies between what he, his doctor, and his parents said, the family was important to accomplish effective treatment. At least the therapy would help "get them off your back." There was family tension to do something different.

As Matt was unsuccessfully "treating" his addiction by trying to control how much of the drug he self-administered, it was clear that a significantly different approach needed to be applied. The patient agreed to include his mother and father in treatment to curtail their intrusiveness, not recognizing the reciprocal nature of the stable pattern they had created. Basically, the intrusiveness involved vigilance borne out of concern. The intervention plan would focus on:

- Parental intrusiveness
- Matt's drug use
- Matt's health risks
- New solutions in a different context for the family

The family business was the glue that held them all together, so a family intervention was consistent with their natural orientation. Family crises were always related to Matt's drug use in the context of the family business; some examples were: his stealing money from the cash register, being rude to customers, or his absenteeism. The usual "solutions" involving threats and infantilizing ultimatums had been unsuccessful.

Intervention Plan

A two-hour meeting was set up that included the clinician, Matt, and his parents. They informed me of their enormous concerns for Matt as well as the constant shortages of money in his cash register. They "fired" him numerous times and rehired him after his sincere promises to reform. Addiction was explained, options were discussed, and doubts were raised by the parents as to whether or not they would be able to change in relation to Matt. Recommended was the following:

- Matt attend NA regularly
- Matt's urine be monitored
- If urine is a positive indicator of drug use, Matt would have two choices: (1) to go into rehab or (2) to quit the family business forever and be stricken from his parents will except for a small amount of money ($1,000).

Matt's parents could not conceive of leaving their assets to Matt, to kill himself with drugs. All were convinced that he was capable of doing such a thing.

Outcome

Within two weeks of the implementation of the plan, Matt's urine tested positive for Quaaludes. A crisis ensued, and the parents struggled over the plan. The father, unknown to all of us, had already purchased plane tickets for he and Matt to leave on a flight to the treatment program at 7 a.m. the next day after our 8 p.m. appointment the night before. After mild protest, Matt went with his father. The entire family participated in one week of live-in treatment of a four-week program. This was of enormous benefit, as a new language of change began to be spoken.

Follow-Up

Treatment continued weekly for six months after return from rehab. Matt lost forty-two pounds and was deeply involved in NA. The parents thrived with their new NAR-ANON contacts. Matt helped open a new family store, and became an accomplished fisherman. Also, Matt embraced the NA twelve steps in a remarkably enthusiastic way. He understood that achieving abstinence was the key to life's new choices. The two-year follow-up saw Matt living independently, drug free, an NA sponsor, and he had maintained appropriate weight loss and expressed gratitude for the intervention.

Case Example 2: The Carter Family

Background Information

At the urging of the youngest child, the five adult children, (twenty-five to forty years old) requested an intervention for their sixty-seven-year-old father. Mr. Carter had been a long-term alcoholic. The children were concerned about mood lability and physical illness in their father. A recent physical exam indicated liver damage. It was mentioned that their mother was extremely angry at their father. The children were all highly motivated to see their father and themselves in treatment. They expressed great pain in watching their father's deterioration.

Assessment

The years of drinking had caused serious health and marital problems. Mr. Carter was unable to appreciate the relationship between his problems and his drinking.

The youngest child, a health professional, had been unsuccessful as the family helper in influencing her father to acknowledge his alcoholism. Her perceived failure to help the family had a significant effect on her personal development. Fortunately, she was able to mobilize the family to permit a professional to penetrate the family's boundary and accept an intervention.

Mr. Carter was an alcoholic for more than fifty years. His drinking increased since an imposed retirement. He worked part-time with one of his sons doing carpentry work. Recently, he partially severed a finger with a power saw and was told during the hospital visit that he had some liver damage by his physician. Any connection to alcohol was ignored. His relationship with Mrs. Carter had deteriorated to the point of severe marital distress and isolation.

Intervention Plan

The intervention was to include all five siblings, two in-laws, the maternal grandmother, a grandchild, and the therapist. The format of the intervention for each was to present Mr. Carter with the following information:

- His or her statement of concern
- A cherished experience with Mr. Carter
- His or her view of his symptoms and diagnosis
- What he or she wants to happen
- What the consequences would be if Mr. Carter should refuse the intervention

The youngest daughter escorted Mr. Carter to my office, where all were waiting. She indicated that they were going to her therapist's office to address issues "only you can help with." Two rehearsals had been conducted, and a treatment program was waiting to receive Mr. Carter. One of the sons had done Mr. Carter's packing. Due to the anger between Mr. Carter and Mrs. Carter, Mrs. Carter was not involved in the intervention. However, she was to be called when we were finished and then brought to my office.

Outcome

The intervention took almost four emotional hours, and Mr. Carter accepted treatment. He was driven by two of his sons to a treatment program an hour away. The treatment program was fitting with his Catholic beliefs and was family oriented. A discounted rate and payment schedule were arranged prior to the intervention, and the staff at the treatment center eagerly awaited Mr. Carter's arrival, despite the lateness of the hour. At the encouragement of the treatment staff, one follow-up session was conducted with the therapist and the treatment center. The purpose was to review the aftercare plan, include Mrs. Carter, and reach closure on issues raised by the intervention.

Follow-Up

Although Mr. Carter had a difficult alcohol detoxification, he embraced the twelve steps with his family. Marital treatment continued for a year after the rehabilitation program. The youngest daughter moved out. Mr. Carter remained sober and an active AA member three years after the intervention.

DISCUSSION OF CASES: WHY INTERVENTIONS WORK

The intervention becomes the integration of many principles of many therapies. The therapist or interventionist draws upon those principles consistent with understanding what a family needs at the moment a family appears, and matches that with the orientation of his or her practice.

In the cases described, the interventionist helped the families develop specific goals and objectives without imposing a requirement that the identified patient do anything. The families were no longer in the position of attempting to alter the behavior of anyone. The therapist sought to help the families develop an alternative to their actions by creating an environment in which new information could be introduced and an invitation for change would be offered.

In looking at families before and after interventions, as with the Best Family and the Carter Family, there is a recognizable shift in communication. Preintervention families such as the Bests and Carters engage in repetitive complaints and demands directed at the using family member. These complaints and demands are ignored. Such a sequence is most familiar to those working with or living in a family with a chemical dependency problem. Affect is intense in preintervention families, with intense emotions expressed to the addict or alcoholic. Of course, the extreme emotion finds no response other than to see it escalate. The family cannot conduct itself in a manner where they expect change when they are bound by the same rules that maintain the problem. The intervention is powerful because it changes the rules in a way consistent with the family's wishes without being punitive or reactive.

Why do interventions seem to work so effectively? First, change comes about very painfully in families with chemical dependence. Prochaska et al. reviews the stages of change with addictive behaviors.[11] The five stages are:

1. precontemplation
2. contemplation
3. preparation
4. action
5. maintenance

The stages of change combined with Gorski's Developmental Model of Recovery gives us some answers.[12] Intervening with an addiction is an active process. That has been the theme of this chapter. Inertia shifts from a body at rest staying at rest to a body in motion staying in motion. Interventions are both process and content simultaneously.

Second, when a family seeks to do something different, it is a powerful sign that a window of opportunity has opened and must be entered rapidly. The family is familiar with stabilizing around dysfunction. Participating in the intervention is a sign that there is a desire to stabilize around change. This is a major shift requiring focused planning and action.

Third, education about chemical dependency is a formable component of any intervention. It is powerful to explain the disease model and to differentiate between the idea of a practicing versus a recovering addict or alcoholic. This allows a reframing of the problem in a way that promotes appropriate helping resources without blaming and judging. Blaming and judging are homeostatic and do not promote change.

Fourth, patterns of interaction can be easily and permanently changed. The silence is broken and new relationships form with different content and process. Just the process of meeting for the intervention planning begins a dramatic change.

INTEGRATIVE MODEL OF INTERVENTION

An especially effective model of intervention is the integrative one suggested by Forman.[13] He has described a nice, inclusive model that incorporates concepts from the above three. The components are as follows:

1. *Phase I:* facing the facts and mobilizing
2. *Phase II:* family education
3. *Phase III:* rehearsal
4. *Phase IV:* the intervention
5. *Phase V:* follow-up

This model provides flexibility integrates principles and techniques base on individual style of therapy while maintaining consistent with intervention concepts discussed.

SUMMARY

The intervention is a powerful way of assisting families to do something very different—helping a chemically dependent family member in treatment. But, most important, success is not defined by that outcome as much as by changing the impact that family member has on the rest of the family. In the absence of that, chemical dependency has often created intractable, habitual problems that persist for many family members for years. The four approaches discussed in this chapter come together as additional tools to place in our clinical tool box in working with chemical dependent families. Through a brief focused process, we construct a therapeutic reality oriented toward change and mutual influence.[14]

More defined research on interventions will provide additional help in refining the process. Clinicians estimate that such interventions are successful a majority of the time. Systematic research would help validate this powerful tool.

REFERENCES

1. Johnson, Veron. (1986). *Intervention.* Minneapolis, MN: Johnson Books, p. 61.

2. Johnson, pp. 11-12.

3. National Federation of Societies for Clinical Social Work. (1994). Fact Sheet.

4. Haley, Jay. (1971). A review of the family therapy field. In J. Haley (Ed.), *Changing families.* New York: Grune and Stratton, pp. 1-12.

5. Lappin, Jay. (1988). Family therapy: A structural approach. In R.A. Dorfman (Ed.), *Paradigms of clinical social work.* New York: Brunner/Mazel, p. 221.

6. Reid, William J. (1988). Brief task-centered treatment. In R.A. Dorfman (Ed.), *Paradigms of Clinical Social Work.* New York: Brunner/Mazel, pp. 196-219.

7. Reid. pp. 196-219.

8. Scapocznik, J., Perez-Vidal A., Hervis, O., and Brickman, A. (1990). Innovations in family therapy: Strategies for overcoming resistance to treatment. In R. Wells and V. Giannetti (Eds.), *Handbook of the brief therapies.* New York: Plenum Press, pp. 93-114.

9. Minuchin, Salvador (1974). *Families and family therapy.* Cambridge, MA: Harvard University Press.

10. Haley, Jay (1976). *Problem-solving therapy.* San Francisco: Jossey-Bass.

11. Prochaska, J.O., DiClemente, C.C., and Norcross, J.C. (1992). In search of how people change: Applications to addictive behaviors. *American Psychologist,* September, pp. 1102-1114.

12. Gorski, T. and Miller, M. (1982). *Learning to live again: Guide for recovery from alcoholism.* Independence, MO: Herald House-Independence Press.

13. Forman, Robert (1987). Circle of care: Confronting the alcoholic's denial. *family therapy networker,* July/August, pp. 34-37.

14. Minuchin, Salvador. (1979). Constructing a therapeutic reality. In E. Kaufman and P. Kaufmam (Eds.), *Family therapy of drug abuse.* New York: Gardner Press, pp. 5-18.

Chapter 8

Legal Strategy

Peggy F. Hora
William G. Schma

Traditionally, judges and other members of the justice system have ignored the underlying disease of addiction when dealing with criminal defendants or family/juvenile court litigants. Court professionals were not equipped, trained, or inclined to be social workers or treatment providers. Treatment and recovery itself was considered either "inappropriate 'in the court setting" or, in the criminal law context, "soft on crime." Few if any understood or acknowledged the relationship between addiction and criminal behavior. The fact that it is ludicrous to send alcoholics or other addicts to jail or prison without the opportunity for treatment was not addressed. The embarrassment of confronting a person's addiction was too much for the court system and, despite the preponderance of evidence of chronic substance abuse available in police reports or probation memos, intervention in the legal system was deemed a matter of personal health and beyond the scope of adjudication.

In the last ten years, two parallel phenomena have emerged, creating an atmosphere in which treatment has become an appropriate and respected alternative to traditional punishment or civil orders. As judges, public defenders, parole officers, prosecuters, and others in the justice system became increasingly frustrated with the ineffectiveness, expense, and inhumanity of using punishment to achieve addiction recovery. At the same time, they were becoming more sophisticated about the disease model and its implications for treatment. As it became clear to them that addiction was primarily a medical issue, albeit a medical issue tossed into the lap of the criminal justice system, it became equally clear that the solutions to this problem were not increased punishment, more prisons, or longer sentences.

The production of court-ordered attendance at twelve-step meetings and referral for treatment became more accepted. However, such judicial referrals were initially unsuccessful because treatment slots were few, waiting lists were long, and cooperation between criminal justice agencies and treatment providers was nonexistent. Judges, probation officers, and parole agents had little understanding of addiction as a chronically relapsing disease. The offenders were "afforded" the opportunity to participate in treatment as an alternative to incarceration and if they "failed," it was their own fault. There was no attempt by the criminal justice system to evaluate the type or duration of treatment, and few parole and probation officers could recognize the cues which could signal relapse and a return to criminal behavior. Judges and other legal professionals experienced a sense of betrayal by defendants who, by their continued use, seemed to be rejecting the gift of treatment. The lens through which the judicial system viewed the defendant was typically of that of an average, normal, responsible adult. The notions of craving and continued use despite adverse consequences never entered into the equation. One positive drug test often resulted in the imposition of extended jail or prison terms. The attitude was, "I gave you a chance; you blew it; now you do time."

Today, as the understanding of the disease of addiction has grown and trust between the recovery community and the courts has developed, the issue of coerced treatment and the responding penal reaction to relapse is changing with positive results. The criminal justice system recognizes a unique ability to motivate a change in an addict shortly after a significant triggering event (such as an arrest), and to compel the addicts to enter and remain in treatment. The traditional goal of the criminal justice system—to deter and punish criminal behavior—and the traditional goals of treatment communities—to decrease problems resulting from substance abuse and to improve the functioning of the patient—have begun to merge. There is a movement among court professionals across the country that employs principles of coerced treatment and utilizes the court system as an intervention tool to motivate recovery.

In some court settings, "criminal defendants" become "drug court patients." Police agencies are sharing block grant monies with drug treatment courts. Judges and other court professionals can be seen lobbying for increased treatment monies. There is a growing symbiotic relationship between the criminal justice and treatment systems which has not heretofore existed.

CRIMINAL SYSTEM CHANGES

Many states include treatment as a part of a sentencing plan for addicted persons who come to the court's attention through criminal behavior. Whether the setting is a probation condition of a driving under the influence/driving while intoxicated (DUI/DWI) arrest or sentencing in a simple drug possession case, addiction treatment has become generally accepted as the only reliable path to crime reduction and recidivism prevention for chemically dependent law breakers.

A national survey of police chiefs found that over half believe they have been unsuccessful in reducing the drug problem. By two to one, the police chiefs favor treatment courts as more effective (59 percent) than jail or prisons (28 percent) for drug users. A fundamental overhaul of the way we deal with the drug problem is overwhelmingly favored by all chiefs.[1] In 1996, *The National Review* declared, "The War on Drugs Is Lost"[2] and criminal justice officials now tend to agree. Current judicial policy supports a model of courtroom intervention, coupled with intensive reporting and treatment through the over 200 "drug courts" established throughout the country. A "drug court" is specifically designated within a jurisdiction to administer cases referred for judicially supervised drug treatment and rehabilitation. The mission of drug courts is to stop the abuse of alcohol and other drugs and its related criminal activity. As a result, more than 28,000 criminal defendants are participating in drug treatment courts in forty-four states.[3]

Jurisdictions without a drug court are also making a significant impact on the drug abuse crime cycle through judicial intervention. At arraignment, the first appearance after arrest, the defendant is informed of the charges and his or her constitutional rights. Bail, bond, or personal recognizance release conditions are set. Electronic monitoring and mandatory attendance at twelve-step self-help group recovery meetings are often required by judges as conditions on sentence reduction release. In addition, the defendant may be ordered to treatment, drug assessment, or drug testing. The judge may also restrict the defendant's permissible travel, communication, or living conditions, such as staying away from drug houses, drug trafficking areas, and drug users. Intervention at this early stage in the criminal justice process has become increasingly effective, and is generally accepted as an appropriate and just response to the arrest.

After assessment, the defendant may be ordered into treatment as a condition of diversion or probation. Diversion is an opportunity for lesser drug offenders without a history of violence to have the arrest or conviction "sealed" after successful completion of a treatment program, payment of fines, AIDS education, etc. In many jurisdictions, a criminal defendant may be eligible to have his or her criminal record sealed, the plea withdrawn, or the charges dismissed upon completion of probation. Release conditions, diversion, and probation which incorporate treatment are some of the tools employed most effectively by judges in courtroom intervention is the center of criminal law.

Alcohol and other drug abuse has come to be seen as a base issue in cases of domestic violence in that treatment for the violence can only begin when the barterer is sober. As a result, the "drug court movement" has expanded to include a growing number of juvenile drug courts which address the cases of minors who are involved in alcohol or other drugs as well as those of parents who are neglecting or abusing their children because of addiction. Judges, defense counsel, prosecutors, and probation officers are more closely examining criminal cases of all types to discover whether there is an underlying alcohol or other drug abuse problem coupled with the criminal behavior.

CIVIL SYSTEM CHANGES

The most profound changes in the recognition of alcohol and other drug abuse in the civil context have come about in child neglect/abuse cases and domestic violence restraining order dockets. As juvenile court professionals discovered that alcohol and other drug problems contributed to the maltreatment of three-fourths of abused children,[4] assessment, abstinence, and treatment began to be required for parents accused of child abuse or neglect. The Department of Social Services (which makes the recommendations to judges about whether parental rights should be terminated and proposes the content of reunification plans) now, more often than not, includes alcohol or other drug abuse treatment as a condition for return of the children.

The recognition of batterers' abuse of alcohol which is present in over half of all domestic violence cases[5] and domestic violence victims' own use and abuse of alcohol and other drugs[6] has led to an understanding of the need for treatment and recovery for the dual problems of violence and substance abuse. Civil restraining orders often include prohibitions on drinking and drug use, as well as restrictions on communications and control with the victim and prohibitions of stalking.

WHY COERCED TREATMENT?

In the old way of thinking about treatment and recovery, it was believed that the alcoholic/addict had to "hit bottom," admit addiction, and overcome denial in order to begin the process of recovery. This model did not lend itself to court-ordered treatment and court-monitored maintenance of sobriety. Some civil libertarians believed that court-ordered, coerced treatment was a violation of due process/equal protection, or reported cruel and unusual punishment and was thus unconstitutional, particularly if a group such as pregnant women were singled out.[7] Others have challenged mandatory attendance at Alcoholics Anonymous meetings as a violation of the First Amendment's freedom of religion clause.[8] Social scientists argued that the treatment community could not demand "voluntary" treatment; so why add resistant bodies to the already overcrowded treatment slots?

By the early 1990s however, work by Dr. Doug Anglin and his colleagues from the University of California at Los Angeles started to show that there was little difference between those who entered treatment voluntarily and those who were court-ordered.[9] Clinicians began to report that by the second or third meeting, they were unable to tell who in a group was court-ordered or who was "voluntary." Indeed, the whole issue of volunteerism in recovery was being reexamined. Some members of Alcoholics Anonymous originally resisted judicial efforts to mandate attendance at twelve-step meetings; in 1990, however, the General Service Office in New York issued "Cooperating with the Court," a guideline for local AA groups.

Some courts have asked successfully recovering criminal defendants to initiate self-help group meetings for current defendants. Others regularly invite volunteers from AA or NA to talk to defendants at arraignment to discuss alternatives to incarceration or conviction. One major hurdle in the recovery process for a criminal defendant is the lack of hope. A court's own "graduates" are the best advertisement for a successful program and the best way to overcome hopelessness.

WHAT'S A JUDGE
(OR OTHER COURT PROFESSIONAL) TO DO?

In the criminal context, the first thing a judge or other drug court professional should do is appreciate the opportunity for intervention created by the defendant's arrest. This crisis could constitute one of the best possible opportunities to call attention to the individual's apparently chronic alcohol or other drug abuse. The court should recognize and acknowledge the family impacts of a chemical dependency, including inherited traits for addiction. It is not unusual for a treatment court judge to ask the criminal defendant who the alcoholic or addict is in the defendant's family—dad or grandma, siblings, aunts, or uncles. Most of the time, the defendant has an immediate answer. This can lead to a discussion of how the defendant came to be in this position and the judge educating the defendant to the role of addiction in the defendant's family history and his or her current position "on the other side of the bench."

The true story of Ruben O. illustrates the point best:

> My name is Ruben O. I am writing to you because I'm
> mentally exhausted every morning. I ask myself, "Why do I

keep opening my eyes?" I have no desire to continue in life. I know the last time I was paroled, I wasn't ready. I feel like I'm on a horrible carousel and I know what's wrong. As far back as I can remember, heroin has been a part of my life.

When I was a small boy, my mother would send me out to play with heroin in my pockets to avoid her being caught in a raid with it. At the age of fourteen, I began using heroin. I've shot heroin with both of my parents. Every crime I've committed was to feed my drug habit. Shortly after I paroled this time, I watched my older sister die due to years of addiction to heroin and methadone. She was the closest thing I had to a mother. After her death, her youngest child began using heroin. I felt numb and lost. I hadn't cried in years. I didn't know I had any cry left in me.

I'm thirty-three years old. I've walked most of the roughest prison yards this state has to offer and seen a whole lot of ugly in my life. To love my sister and watch her baby begin using was all I could stand. I wanted so bad to help her. I know the loneliness my niece was feeling.

I know better than anybody what is wrong with me. I know what kind of help I need, but nobody is listening to me. I've presented a couple long-term drug programs to my PD [public defender]. . . . He cannot relay how I feel in my heart or what I've seen and endured that has brought me to this point in my life.

. . . I am tired. I prefer to go no further in life rather than to continue on and watch my addiction destroy what is left of my life. I don't know how to beg for help any louder or harder. I am writing you with a sincere plea to intercede to help me receive treatment. I am not scared of prison. There are no surprises there for me. What I am afraid of is going and returning the same as always.

. . . If I fail to complete this program, nobody will lose but me. I have no push left. I need the courts to help me regain my sanity and be able to live with me and face life on its own terms.

Not everyone reaches court with the understanding of Ruben O. but, with successful intervention by the court system, many of the Rubens who come through the court system everyday can recover. Applying the standards and principles which have been developed by drug court professionals themselves, criminal courts are becoming an important part of the road to recovery for many people.

TREATMENT COURT ELEMENTS

The National Association of Drug Court Professionals has defined a drug court and articulated the critical elements which make up a drug court. Among them are the following:

- The first element is the integration of alcohol and other drug treatment services with justice system case processing. A non-adversarial approach whereby prosecution and defense counsel promote public safety of the defendant while protecting the due rights.
- Early determination of eligibility so that participants are quickly placed in a drug court program.
- Access to a continuum of alcohol and other drug treatment and rehabilitation services. (In fact, a criminal defendant may never have been habilitated in the first place.)
- Required abstinence monitored by frequent alcohol and other drug testing.
- A coordinated follow-up strategy governing the participants' compliance whereby addiction is recognized as a chronic, relapsing condition. This is the most telling differences between a treatment court and a traditional criminal court.
- Frequent, ongoing judicial interaction with each drug court participant.
- Regular status hearings which provide the court with information necessary to ensure compliance as well as encouragement and, when necessary, appropriate sanctions.
- Effective planning and ongoing evaluation as the measure of the program's overall effectiveness. Evaluations include both process and outcome evaluations. For example, have services

been implemented as intended and have participants reduced their criminal activities and recidivism?

- Continuing interdisciplinary education of judges, counsel, probation, or other supervisory personnel and treatment providers.
- Partnerships with public agencies and community-based organizations. Such partnerships generate long-term support for drug court programs and enhance the court's effectiveness.

These key components and operational standards are still in the developmental stage as judges and others involved in treatment courts realize the need for them. While many of these drug court principles and components are considered universal, it is clear that treatment courts are varied and diverse in their application so as to reflect the needs and the political realities of their particular communities.

REMAINING QUESTIONS

As judges move away from the traditional role of the impartial and aloof arbiter to that of an enthusiastic and involved member of a defendant's treatment team, a philosophical mind shift must take place. Traditional jurisprudence is formalistic, logical, and mechanical. Emphasis is placed on the process of finding the most appropriate law or legal principle and applying it to the problem at hand. The impact on those affected by the process is not considered. However, "therapeutic jurisprudence" is replacing traditional jurisprudence where a physical addiction is present. *Webster's Dictionary* defines "therapeutic" as "of or relating to the treatment of disease or disorders by remedial agents or methods; curative, medicinal."[10] *Black's Law Dictionary* defines "jurisprudence" as "the philosophy of law, or the science which treats of the principles of positive law and legal relations."[11] These definitions may be aptly summarized as a curative system, body or philosophy of law.

The term "therapeutic jurisprudence" was first used in 1987 by David B. Wexler, Professor of Law at the University of Arizona, primarily to describe the events taking place in mental health hearings. Wexler and his partner, Bruce Winick from the University of

Miami, have noted that the field of mental health law had developed based on a constitutional foundation that emphasized protection of personal rights of the mental health patients. However, that foundation was deteriorating, and the vigor which originally infused mental health law had been lost. They explored the extent to which substantive rules, legal procedures, and the roles of lawyers and judges produce therapeutic or antitherapeutic consequences.

This notion is extremely useful in the criminal law context when dealing with alcoholics and other addicts. The traditional role of a defense attorney is to get the client "off," if possible. When the client is an alcoholic or addict who already in denial, looking for procedural loopholes to avoid punishment is certainly antitherapeutic and most likely codependent. The prosecution, traditionally, does not consider the factors making up the individual, but merely the facts that constitute the offense. The judge who, in sentencing, orders only jail time in an institution where there is no treatment in-custody, or who merely gives credit for time served and offers no recovery tools as conditions of probation, is ignoring the root cause of the problem and is inviting antitherapeutic consequences.

By contrast, therapeutic jurisprudence provides an interdisciplinary, empirical, and international orientation that seeks to sensitize legal policymakers to the impact of legal rules and procedures. Judges and other legal professionals practicing in courtrooms in which the cases are viewed through the therapeutic lens balance public safety, the defendants' rights, and the impact of doing business as usual. Is it antitherapeutic for a criminal defendant to be allowed to plead "no contest" rather than guilty to a crime? Is it anti-therapeutic to ignore the underlying problem of substance abuse? Is it therapeutic to require the defendant admit his or her addiction and take steps to recover from it? Treatment court professionals and other judges trying to develop new solutions to the problems of addiction and criminal behavior use the therapeutic lens and recognize that recovery requires no less than a complete life change. As Ruben O. said so eloquently, "I am not scared of prison. There are no surprises for me there. What I'm afraid of is going and returning the same as always."

Drug treatment courts and other judges using therapeutic jurisprudence are part of a growing, new phenomenon which will eventually evolve into a system of community courts. DUI courts, juvenile treatment courts, domestic violence courts, and even "deadbeat dad" courts are being created to reflect community concerns. When the entire court system sees itself as reflective of the surrounding community's concerns and priorities, community participation in and support of the court system increases. Community-based court programs now have a communication vehicle that, heretofore has not existed. As community policing, community prosecuting, and restorative justice principles are employed by a community in cooperation with the local courts, the real solutions to problems confronting us will be revealed. A lingering question remains in the minds of some when confronted with the issue of treatment courts and community justice—is this an appropriate role for the judge, for the attorneys, for probation, and for the courts? The response must be: If not us, who? If not now, when?

REFERENCES

1. Hart, Peter D. Research Associates, "Drugs & Crime Across America: Police Chiefs Speak Out," Police Foundation and Drug Strategies (1996).

2. "The War on Drugs Is Lost." *The National Review*, July 1, 1996.

3. Navarro, Mireya, "Drug Courts Record Tentative Successes in Hard-Fought War," *Daily Journal* (October 18, 1996).

4. Children in alcohol-abusing families are 3.6 times more likely to be victims of maltreatment, according to the National Center on Child Abuse and Neglect (NCCAN). Alcohol and other drug problems in the family contributed to the abuse of 78 percent of maltreated children. Maltreatment was defined as physical, sexual, or emotional abuse as well as physical, educational, or emotional neglect. "Children in Alcohol Abusing Homes Suffer More Maltreatment," 6 *Prevention Pipeline* (November/December 1993) 6:29.

5. In a study cited in "Making the Link: Domestic Violence & Alcohol and Other Drugs" published by the Center for Substance Abuse Prevention (CSAP) (Spring 1995), alcohol was present in ore than 50 percent of all incidents of domestic violence.

6. Alcoholic women have been found to be significantly more likely to have experienced negative verbal conflict with spouses than were nonalcoholic women. They were also significantly more likely to have experienced a range of moderate and severe physical violence.

7. See, e.g., Moss, Kary L., "Forced Drug or Alcohol Treatment for Pregnant and Postpartum Women: Part of the Solution or Part of the Problem?", *New England Journal on Criminal and Civil Confinement 17* (Winter 1991) :1 and Chavkin, Wendy, "Mandatory Treatment for Drug Use During Pregnancy," *Journal of the American Medical Association 266* (September 18, 1991):1556.

8. Jordan, Hallye, "State Workers Call Drug Treatment Religious Bias," *San Francisco Daily Journal* (December 14, 1995).

9. Anglin, M. Douglas and Yih-ing Hser, "Legal Coercion and Drug Abuse Treatment: Research Findings and Social Policy Implications," *Handbook of Drug Control in the United States*, James A. Inciardi, Ed. (1990) and Anglin, M. Douglas, Mary-Lynn Brecht, and Ebrahim Maddahian, "Pretreatment Characteristics and Treatment Performance of Legally Coerced Versus Voluntary Methadone Maintenance Admissions," 27 *Criminology* 537 (1989); and, DuPlessis, Helen, "The Effectiveness of Coercion in Treatment Pregnant Substance Using Women" Conference Paper, The Interface Between Treatment and Punishment in Controlling Illegal Drug Use, RAND, (April 26-27, 1991).

10. *Webster's Third New International Dictionary*, 1976.

11. *Black's Law Dictionary*, Fourth Edition, revised, 1968.

RESOURCES

National Association of Drug Court Professionals
Hon. Jeffrey Tauber, President
901 N. Pitt Street #300
Alexandria, VA 22314
Office: 703-706-0576 FAX:703-706-0565

California Association of Drug Court Professionals
Hon. Steve Marcus, President
213-974-6111

American University Drug Court Clearinghouse
Carolyn Cooper, Department of Justice Programs
Brandywine #6C, 4400 Massachusetts Avenue NW
Washington, DC 20016
Office: 202-885-2875 FAX: 202-885-2885

Center for Judicial Education and Research (CJER)
Karen Moen, Drug Courts Programs
303 Second Street, North Tower, #450
San Francisco, CA 94107
Office: 415-356-6430 FAX: 415-356-6445

Drug Courts Program Office
Marilyn Roberts, Director
Office of Justice Programs
633 Indiana Avenue, NW
Washington, DC 20531
Office: 202-616-5001 FAX: 202-307-2019

Felix Stumpf
Drug Courts Program Attorney
National Judicial College
University of Nevada
Reno, NV 89557
800-25-JUDGE   FAX: 702-784-1253

BIBLIOGRAPHY

Finn, Peter and Andrea K. Newlyn. "Miami Drug Court Gives Drug Defendants a Second Chance," *NIJ Journal* (November 1993).
————. "Miami's Drug Court," *National Institute of Justice NCJ,* no. 142412 (June 1993).
Goldkamp, John S. and Doris Weiland. "Assessing the Impact of Dade County's Felony Drug Court," *National Institute of Justice NCJ,* no. 145302 (December 1993).
Goldkamp, John S., "Justice and Treatment Innovation: The Drug Court Movement," National Institute of Justice NCJ, no. 149260 (October 1994).
Lehman, Jack, "The Movement Towards Therapeutic Jurisprudence," X *NJC Alumni* 13 (Spring 1995).
McColl, William D., "Baltimore City's Drug Treatment Court: Theory and Practice in an Emerging Field," 55 *Maryland Law Review* 467 (1996).
Prendergast, Michael L. and Thomas H. Maugh II, "Drug Courts: Diversion That Works," *The Judges Journal* (Summer 1995).
Setterberg, Fred, "Drug Court," *California Lawyer* 58 (May 1994).
Smith, Barbara E., Rober C. Davis, Sharon R. Goretsky, Arthur J. Lurigio, and Susan Popkin. "Drug Night Courts: How Feasible Are They?" 1 *BJA Bulletin* 1 NCJ, no. 142725 (July 1993).
Tauber, Jeffrey S., "Drug Courts: A Judicial Manual," *CJER Journal* (Special Issue, Summer 1994).
Zimring, Franklin E. "Drug Treatment as a Criminal Sanction," *University of Colorado Law Review,* 64 (1993).
————. "Do Drugs. Do Time: An Evaluation of the Maricopa County Demand Reduction Program," National Institute of Justice NCJ 149016 (October 1994).
————."Drug Court Judges Cite Need to Blend Strictness, Compassion," 2 *CJN Drug Letter* 1 (January 1994).
————. "Drug Courts: A Profile of Operational Programs," The American University National Symposium on the Implementation and Operation of Drug Courts (December 3-5, 1995).
————. "Drug Courts: Information on a New Approach to Address Drug-Related Crime, " U.S. General Accounting Office, GAO/GGD-95-159BR (May 1995).
————. "Drug Courts: The Next Steps—Conference Proceedings," National Institute of Justice (December 1-4, 1993).

————. "Drug Night Courts: The Cook County Experience," Bureau of Justice Assistance NJC 147185 (August 1994).

————. "Self-Assessment Guide," National Association of Drug Court Professionals (1996).

————. "Special Drug Courts," Bureau of Justice Assistance, (November 1993).

————. "Success of New Drug Court Attributed to Planning Process," 2 *CJN Drug Letter* 5 (June 1994).

————. "Summary Experience of the Drug Court Experience," Office of Justice Programs, American University, (October 1996).

————. "Treatment Drug Courts," Bureau of Justice Assistance (September 1994).

BIBLIOGRAPHY ON COURT-ORDERED/ COERCED TREATMENT

Anglin, M. Douglas and Thomas H. Maugh II. "Overturning Myths About Coerced Drug Treatment," (Citation).

Anglin, M. Douglas and Yih-ing Hser. "Legal Coercion and Drug Abuse Treatment: Research Findings and Social Policy Implications," *Handbook of Drug Control in the United States*, James A. Inciardi, Ed. (1990).

Anglin, M. Douglas, Mary-Lynn Brecht, and Ebrahim Maddahian, "Pretreatment Characteristics and Treatment Performance of Legally Coerced Versus Voluntary Methadone Maintenance Admissions," 27 *Criminology* 537 (1989).

Aukerman, Robert B. Consensus Panel Chair, "Combining Substance Abuse Treatment with Intermediate Sanctions for Adults in the Criminal Justice System, Treatment Improvement Protocol (TIP) (1994).

Brecht, Mary-Lynn, M. Douglas Anglin, and Jung-chi Wang. "Treatment Effectiveness for Legally Coerced Versus Voluntary Methadone Maintenance Clients," 19 *Am J Drug Alcohol Abuse* 89 (1993).

Chavkin, Wendy. "Mandatory Treatment for Drug Use During Pregnancy," 266 *J Am Med Assn* 1556 (September 18, 1991).

DeLeon, G. "Legal Pressure in Therapeutic Communities," *J of Drug Issues* (1988).

DuPlessis, Helen. "The Effectiveness of Coercion in Treating Pregnant Substance Using Women," Conference Paper, The Interface Between Treatment and Punishment in Controlling Illegal Drugs, RAND, (April 26-27, 1991).

Gallant, D.M. "Evaluation of Compulsory Treatment of the Alcoholic Municipal Court Offender," In *Recent Advances in Studies of Alcoholism: An Interdisciplinary Symposium,* N.K. Mello and J.H. Mendelson, Eds. (1970).

Garcia, Sandra A. and Ingo Keilitz. "Involuntary Civil Commitment of Drug-Dependent Persons With Special Reference to Pregnant Women," 15 *MPDLR* 418 (July-August 1991).

Leukenfeld, Carl G. and Frank M. Tims, Eds., "Compulsory Treatment for Drug Abuse," 25 *Int J of the Add* 621 (1990).

Leukenfeld, Carl G. and Frank M. Tims, Eds., *Compulsory Treatment of Drug Abuse: Research and Clinical Practice*, National Institute of Drug Abuse NIH Pub. No. (ADM) 88-1578 (1994).

Mathiew, Deborah, "Mandating Treatment for Pregnant Substance Abusers: A Compromise," 14 *Pol and the Life Sci* 199 (August 1995).

Moss, Kary L., "Forced Drug or Alcohol Treatment for Pregnant and Postpartum Women: Part of the Solution or Part of the Problem?" *New Eng J On Crim & Civil Confine* 1 (Winter 1991).

Newman, Robert G. "The Argument Against Long-Term Addiction Treatment in Prison," 5 *Drug For* 369 (1976-1977).

Platt, J.J., Gerhard Buhringer, Charles D. Kaplan, Barry S. Brown, and Daniel O. Taube, "Prospects and Limitations of Compulsory Treatment for Drug Addiction," 18 *J of Drug Iss* 505 (1988).

Satel, Sally, "Interview," *The Facts About Tobacco, Alcohol, and Other Drugs*, University of Florida Brain Institute (Spring 1996).

Schottenfeld, Richard S., "The Troubling Question of Court-Ordered Treatment," *Washington Post Health* (Oct. 23, 1990).

Walsh, D.C., R.W. Hingson, D.M. Merrigan, S. Morlock-Levinson, L.A. Cupples, T. Heeren, G.A. Coffman, C.A. Becker, and T.A. Barker, "Randomized Trial of Treatment Options for Alcohol Abusing Workers," 325 *New Eng J of Med* 775 (1991).

See also: *In re: Tanya P* Index No. 530069/93, Supreme Court of New York, opinion of J. Kristin Booth Glen in which the judge denied the retention of a pregnant woman in Bellevue to "protect her fetus" under the Mental Hygiene Law of New York.

Symposium: *Pregnancy and Substance Abuse, Politics and the Life Sciences* Beech Tree Publishing, (March 1996).

Chapter 9

Professional Intervention in the One-Stop Reemployment/Social Services Center

Deborah G. Wright

Integrated one-stop reemployment and social services centers present a unique opportunity for alcohol and drug abuse intervention in the public services setting. An outgrowth of bipartisan Congressional welfare and workforce reform initiatives, these multiservice centers involve the co-location of personnel from two or more agencies serving the unemployed, the underemployed, the disabled, and similar populations. Among the most common one-stop partners are employment departments, private industry councils/job-training partnerships, food stamp and welfare programs, community college skills centers, child protective services, and community corrections. Hence, people no longer must travel to five or more locations to gain needed assistance to become self-sufficient.

When co-located, one-stop agencies are increasingly coordinating services to minimize red tape, reduce costs, and further extend services. Partnering agencies, especially in satellite and rural centers, often share, subcontract, or cross-train personnel to be able to provide interagency information, conduct intakes, and deliver emergency services. Federally approved waivers have further encouraged coordination by allowing certain states to relax their program criteria in return for better results. Oregon has taken the lead in this initiative, with six other states achieving similar waivers in fall 1997. By shortening the time before reemployment or self-sufficiency, these states will reduce overall caseloads and the needed federal funding.

THE POPULATION

A large percentage of the individuals needing emergency social and reemployment services have chronic alcohol and drug problems. Case workers at the Newmark Career and Opportunity One Stop in Coos Bay, Oregon, estimate that chronic substance abuse is an issue in the homes of as many as eight of every ten welfare recipients. Case workers in the local Services to Families and Children program report a confirmed methamphetamine involvement of 56 percent in 184 open cases of child abuse or neglect, and alcohol or other drug abuse in over 90 percent of the remaining caseload.

The coincidence of substance abuse and the need for social services is not surprising considering that the most common indicator of chemical dependency is not the presence of the drug but rather the continuing and accelerating increase of crises in an individual's life. These become more evident as dependency progresses. For example, alcohol, marijuana, or methamphetamine use as a teenager results in an inability to learn and problems in school, as well as teen pregnancy, dropping out of school, and bare survival in a low-paying job. As adults, drug-induced mood swings result in behavior problems on the job—anger, depression, accidents, assaults, insomnia, drowsiness, tardiness, absenteeism—and the threat of job loss, increasing the reliance on alcohol and drugs to ease the stress.

The stress and drug effects cause family problems, eventually resulting in disputes, spousal or child abuse, runaways, separation, and divorce. These in turn cause the need for emergency food, shelter, and welfare services. Accidents, citations for driving while intoxicated (DWI), or driving under the influence of a chemical (DUI) cause suspension of driver's licenses. Individuals who cannot afford, repair, maintain, or insure their vehicles lose the transportation necessary to travel to a job. Lack of money for necessities, and the compulsion for more drugs results in theft or drug dealing, and eventual legal problems, including incarceration, affecting not only the self-sufficiency of the individual, but the family as well. Thus the problems multiply. Eventually, the individual ends up as a client of not one but several social services agencies.

In many cases, economic and personal problems lead to drug abuse, which causes problems to worsen in a synergistic dynamic.

Regardless of the cause, most social workers have found that the cycle of poverty and crime can be significantly reduced if individuals with alcohol and drug abuse issues are identified and motivated to seek treatment.

Until co-location of agencies in one-stop centers, people with alcohol or drug addictions could access emergency assistance from one agency after another, always avoiding facing the primary cause of their problems. A drug-addicted mother could visit one organization and receive food stamps, which she would immediately sell for drugs, go to another agency for milk and cheese for her young children, which again would be sold for drugs, and eventually to a third agency for an emergency food basket to finally feed the hungry children. Lack of communication among agencies has resulted in enabling the substance abuse to continue and its damaging effects to increase. "Service hopping" has become a skill that a child learns from parent, and client from client. Clients learn "the talk"—how to tell each agency whatever story will help them gain the services provided there.

Without shared information, agency staff cannot intervene to stop the downward cycle, and the public will continue to pay the high price of addiction. However, with co-location and integrated service delivery, teams or "conciliation boards" can meet to discuss common clients. In these meetings, the stories provided by the clients to each agency are often so radically different that it is difficult to believe they are discussing the same client. Once the whole picture is evident, an appropriate plan can be developed. Further agency enabling is prevented.

More important, because such problems involve many aspects of a person's life, a multidisciplinary approach is needed involving not only treatment but coordination of ancillary services, including job preparation and placement. Such services are most effective when delivered simultaneously through an individualized plan.

MAINTAINING CONFIDENTIALITY

Privacy regulations restrict communication of certain confidential information across agency lines. However, barriers to integrated client strategies are more often organizational and cultural than legal.

As the director of one site-integration team states, "Overcoming staff resistance to shared client information is not unlike a marriage. It takes time to develop confidence, trust, and cooperation."

Several intervention approaches that do not compromise client confidentiality are being employed successfully by social services and reemployment centers that have achieved coordinated service delivery.

Common Application Form

In an integrated one stop, a common application form may be employed to assist individuals to access the range of services located at the site. When confidential information is requested, the individual must sign a consent form if such information is to be shared across agency lines. The form must allow the individual to designate or check off each agency with which the confidential information may be shared. When shown the option of applying for services separately, filling out the multiple forms, and when told of the advantages of a cross-team plan, most clients readily sign the consent. In this case, all staff members who would be able to access the data have signed confidentiality agreements with their agencies, and have pledged to maintain the confidentiality of all client information. The agencies have signed confidentiality agreements among themselves, and commit to train staffs on confidentiality regulations.

Once the client has signed the application for multiagency services, allowing for the sharing of information among agencies, and the initial assessments are completed, a team meets to develop a service plan for the individual or family.

At such meetings, it may become apparent that a client has greater problems than recognized. A case worker may share that the individual was aggressive with staff; a trainer may share that the individual missed classes; the counselor may share that the children have been removed from the home. An emergency worker may share that emergency housing is needed.

In most cases involving a chemical dependency, there is denial that the alcohol or drug use is causing or increasing the number of problems. A worker meets with the client to develop appropriate strategies to move toward self-sufficiency. The worker discusses the recurring problems and the need to address whatever is causing them, explaining that medical problems, heavy alcohol use, drug use, and depression can all be causes of such problems. A confidential screening with an alcohol and drug counselor is suggested to "rule out the possibility." If the individual refuses, the worker suggests that if problems continue, the individual will promise to consider having a screening. When future problems recur, the team leader and, if appropriate, one or more members of the team, meet with the individual and share their observations in a nonconfrontational intervention procedure. The workers strive to express their concern for the client's well-being, establish mutual respect, and maintain the client's dignity throughout the conversation. The team continues to meet regularly to review the client's progress.

Universal Alcohol and Drug Screening

Under new federal regulations, all work-capable welfare recipients must participate in the JOBS (job readiness and placement) program. In Oregon, beginning July 1, 1997, as the result of a federal agreement, all JOBS participants who receive cash benefits must complete the Substance Abuse Subtle Screening Inventory (SASSI). If the SASSI score is "hot," the individual is referred to an alcohol and drug counselor for a clinical assessment, intervention, and treatment. Individuals continue to receive welfare benefits to the percentage that they participate in the required JOBS services, including treatment. If treatment is 40 percent of a client's time commitment, and he or she refuses treatment, the client loses 40 percent of his or her benefits. Congress is examining this program as a model for all welfare recipients.

Alcohol and drug screening can be required by programs which place clients with employers for whom alcohol and drug testing is mandated by law, as well as those who for safety or liability reasons require workers to be alcohol- and drug-free.

A common misconception is that treatment only succeeds when it is initiated by the person with the dependency; however, experience with employer interventions shows the opposite is true. Whenever continued employment (pay and benefits) is contingent on the employee's abstinence and participation in treatment and a twelve-step program, the intervention is more successful in achieving long-term recovery than any other form of intervention. Success rates of 80 percent or higher are commonly reported by industry journals.

Volunteered Information

Often the spouse, partner, parent, or child, and sometimes even the substance abuser, will volunteer information to a case worker about a drug or alcohol problem in the home. The professional can then explain that addiction often causes financial, legal, family, and medical problems, rather than the other way around, and that confidential help is available. If the individual wants help, the professional can refer the person to the appropriate treatment provider. In a one stop, it is often a walk with the client to the other side of the building to meet with an addictions counselor to discuss the situation.

Many times, public employees are caught in a "confidance" trap, where a client will preface discussion of alcohol or drug abuse with, "This is confidential, you cannot tell anyone." If the situation is repeated on the second visit, the employee should communicate that he or she feels strongly that such confidentiality is not in the best interest of the client. The employee should urge the client to accompany him or her to meet someone who is more knowledgeable and who can help: "You are asking me for help and that is what I want to give you, but you are tying my hands by asking me not to tell anyone. I am not the one who can help you. I know you want help, and that is why you are telling me this. Now, let's go get help."

Clients rarely refuse when the worker expresses such concern and accompanies the individual to the counselor's office.

INTERVENING WITH CARE

Case workers, trainers, and service personnel should never attempt to diagnose a chemical dependency, or to accuse the individual of substance abuse, but should address the obvious life problems, such as continued accidents, DUIs, inability to hold a job, problems in the home, missed appointments with case workers, etc. This can be accomplished through a four-step informal intervention process best remembered for the letters CARE.

The acronym CARE stands for the four key steps: communicate, affirm, respond, enact. The strategy is to communicate genuine concern and a sense of urgency to address the problems in the person's life, whatever the cause.

Since the ultimate purpose of the intervention is to recover the client and help him or her to become fully self-sufficient, a sense of care should pervade the intervention—respect for the rights of the client and maintain the confidentiality, and most of all, care for the welfare of the client. The intervention requires a delicate balance of communication, concern, and corrective action.

An interactive intervention technique, CARE provides a template for both formal and informal behavior and addiction interventions. Since its development in 1984, CARE has been adapted for use in clinical, impaired professional, employer, student assistance, and family problem interventions.

Step 1: Communicate the Facts
and Your Concern About a Problem

The purpose of this step is for the professional to initiate a dialogue and create receptiveness. This can be done best by first asking the client about his or her progress and challenges. After listening, the worker shares knowledge about the specific problem with the client, expresses concern, and invites a discussion. For example, this might be that the client has missed the last two appointments, or that the worker notices the client's DUI in the paper the previous week: "Saw your name in the paper, John. There is a lot happening in your life right now. Want to talk about it?"

Step 2: Affirm the Client

The purpose of this step is to hear the client's explanation and diffuse any anger. By listening well and rephrasing what the client has said, the professional reassures the client that what he or she says is important. Thus, a willingness is created on the part of the client to hear the professional's response.

The client may give an unbelievable explanation for the poor performance or other problems. Substance abuse will cause people to minimize or deny the complications of the drugs. Rephrasing the client's explanation allows the professional to clarify what was heard, to make a note of the explanation, and to show the client that the professional is listening. It has the added benefit of letting the client hear what he or she has just said, and it usually does not sound quite as good. It is important that the professional not appear to be mimicking, criticizing, or questioning the validity of the client's statement, but rather trying to be accurate about what was heard. In this way, the client maintains dignity and a willingness to continue the dialogue. It is important that the professional be able to empathize with the client's predicament and express that empathy. "You have worked hard to get this far. It must be very hard for you . . . I know you can't want it to keep going like this."

One addictions counselor gives a closed orientation to alcohol and drug services to all clients of a one stop, sharing that she is in recovery and wants people to know that she understands, not just as a professional, but as one who has been there: "If you are someone with a drug or alcohol problem in yourself or your family, I want you to know you are not alone. Many people have the same problems. I genuinely care about you. I want you to do well because I live in this community with my family. I want you to succeed. I want you to own the home next to mine and for us to raise our kids together in a healthy environment." There is no substitute for talking to people "where they are at."

Step 3: Respond to the Problem at Hand

The purpose of this step is to refocus the discussion on the immediate problem(s) and avoid diversions inherent in discussing the client's explanation (whether valid or not). Refocusing is best accomplished by restating the performance or other problem at hand and its likely impacts on the client and the client's self-sufficiency goals. At this point, the worker stresses the need for the client to find the real cause of his or her problems so that they do not continue to make life miserable. Here it is useful to suggest a number of possible causes for the types of problems or behaviors the individual is facing: "I don't know what is causing you all these problems. They could be due to any number of things, medical problems, alcohol or drugs, depression—whatever. But you need to find out, and to do whatever is necessary to take care of it before it gets the best of you and your family."

Step 4: Enact a Referral

The purpose of this step is to bring the discussion to a close by suggesting a referral and offering to help the client gain information which might be useful. This step sets in motion a process for referral, treatment and follow-up care. The worker suggests that, "If it were me, I would want to rule out mental or physical causes, including chemical interaction. There is someone here at the center (or nearby) that is experienced in these things and can answer a lot of questions. It is completely confidential." The worker says he or she has some extra time and would be willing to walk over to introduce them. If the client suggests another time, the worker agrees and gives the client a card with the person's name and number to call if there is an emergency. Usually a goodbye is followed by, "There is no reason to go through this kind of mess if you can find out why and stop it. Problems like these can ruin your life."

AFTER THE INTERVENTION

The worker makes a note of the conversation and the informal referral and continues to monitor the client. If future problems arise, the worker offers to contact the counselor for the client and to have the counselor call him or her to answer their questions.

If further problems are brought to the team, the worker may elect to conduct a more formal intervention with staff from other agencies who share the same client or family. The team decides in advance the best way to motivate the client to take advantage of the treatment service available. Where appropriate and within the law, restriction of services is discussed. In the team intervention, the same four steps are followed, with each team member offering his or her observations and their concerns to the client. The last step usually contains the options, including the availability of treatment, and where appropriate, the potential loss of services if treatment is refused.

STAFF DEVELOPMENT

Organizations considering one-stop participation should place a high priority on training staff to acquaint them with the rules of confidentiality and disclosure. Shared staff development and cross training will help build the trust among professionals to develop shared strategies. All staff need to know how to initiate discussions with clients without accusing them of drug abuse or attempting to diagnose a chemical dependency, and to be trained in nonconfrontational communication strategies, such as the CARE intervention method. Moreover, it is critical that one-stop staffs learn how to express sincere compassion and concern while employing the "incentives" that will motivate a client to seek and participate fully in treatment.

BIBLIOGRAPHY

Wright, Bob, and Wright, Deborah George. (1991). *It's your business—Intervention for a drug-free workplace.* Minneapolis, MN: Hazelden.

Wright, Bob, and Wright, Deborah George. (1990). *Dare to confront: How to intervene when someone you care about has an alcohol or other drug problem.* New York: Master Media.

Appendix A

Selected Resources: Books

Bissel, L. and Haberman, P.W. (1984). *Alcoholism in the professions.* New York: Oxford University Press.

Crosby, L.R. and Bissel, L. (1989). *To care enough: Intervention with chemically dependent colleagues.* Minneapolis: Johnson Institute.

Drews, T.R. (1980). *Getting them sober.* Plainfield, NJ: Bridge Publishing.

Drews, T.R. (1987). *Getting your children sober: A no-fault guide for parents and professionals.* South Plainfield, NJ: Bridge Publishing, Inc..

Edens, K., Muldoon, J., Sternov, R., and Murck, M. (1987). *How to use intervention in your profession.* Minneapolis: Johnson Institute.

Gentilello, L.M. and Duggan, P. (1993). *Treating alcohol problems: Marital and family interventions.* New York: Guilford Press.

Harris, V.A. (1990). *Treatment choices for alcoholism and substance abuse.* Lexington, KY: Lexington Books.

Johnson Institute Books. (1987). *The family enablers*, revised edition. Minneapolis: Johnson Institute.

Johnson Institute Books. (1987). *How to use intervention in your professional practice.* Minneapolis: Johnson Institute.

Johnson Institute Books. (1987). *Recovery of chemically dependent families*, revised edition. Minneapolis: Johnson Institute.

Johnson Institute Books. (1987). *Chemical dependence and recovery: A family affair*, revised edition. Minneapolis: Johnson Institute.

Johnson, V. (1973). *I'll quit tomorrow.* New York: Harper and Row Publishers.

Johnson, V. (1986). *Intervention: How to help someone who doesn't want help.* Minneapolis: Johnson Institute Books.

Meagher, M.D. (1987). *Beginning of a Miracle: How to intervene with the addicted or alcoholic person.* Pompano Beach, CA: Health Communications, Inc.

O'Neill, J. and O'Neill, P. (1989). *How to get help when someone else's drinking or drugging is hurting you.* Austin, TX: Creative Assistance Press.

O'Neill, J. and O'Neill, P. (1992). *Concerned intervention: When your loved one won't quit alcohol or drugs.* Oakland, CA: New Harbinger Publications, Inc.

Rogers, R.L. and McMillin, C.S. (1988). *Don't help: A positive guide to working with the alcoholic.* New York: Bantam Books.

Schaefer, D. (1987). *Choices and consequences: What to do when a teenager uses alcohol/drugs.* Minneapolis: Johnson Institute.

Schwebel, M. Skorina, J., and Schoener, G. (1988). *Assisting impaired psychologists.* Washington, DC: American Psychological Association.

Sullivan, E.J., Bissell, L., and Williams, E. (1988). *Chemical dependency in nursing: The deadly diversion.* Redwood City, CA: Addison-Wesley Publishing Company.

Wright, C. (Ed.) (1989). *Alcoholism and chemical dependency in the workplace.* Philadelphia: Hanley and Belfus.

Wright, D.G. (1992). *Dare to confront: How to intervene when someone you care about has an alcohol or other drug problem.* New York: Master Media, 1990. New York: Dell.

Wright, D.G. (1993). *Creating and maintaining the drug-free workforce.* New York: McGraw-Hill.

Appendix B

Selected Resources: Videos

The following videos can be ordered through the Hazelden 1997 Clinician's Catalog (phone 1-800-328-9000):

- *Structured Intervention—How to Deal with the Addict in Your Life* (1991) Wilton Media Inc.
- The Back to Reality Series with Hugh Downs (1988) (three videos)
    Back to Reality
    Enabling
    Intervention
    Produced by the Johnson Institute
- *The Invisible Line*
    Gerald T. Rogers Productions, Inc., 1988.

The following videos can be ordered through FMS Productions 1997 Catalog (phone: 1-800-421-4609):

- *Family Intervention: A New Approach*
    with Dr. Dan Budenz and Paul Williams
- *Intervention and Recovery*
- *Guidelines for Helping the Alcoholic with Father Martin*

The following video can be ordered through Coronet/MTI Film and Video (phone: 1-800-621-2131):

- *Taking Action: Substance Abuse in the Workplace* (1989)
    Locke Bryan and the Texas Producers Group

Other videos from the Johnson Institute in Minnesota (1-800-321-5165):

- *The Intervention*
- *Choices and Consequences: Intervention with Youth in Trouble with Alcohol/Drugs*
- *Intervention: How to Help Someone Who Doesn't Want Help*

Appendix C

Selected Resources: Organizations

Al-Anon Family Group
World Service Office
P.O. Box 862
Midtown Station
New York, NY 10018
1-800-344-2666

Alcoholics Anonymous (AA)
World Service, Inc.
468 Park Avenue, South
New York, NY 10016
212-870-3400

American Bar Association
Commission on Lawyer Assistance
541 N. Fairbanks Court
Chicago, IL 60611
312-988-5359
  • Contact Person: Donna Spilis

American Dental Association
211 E. Chicago Avenue
Chicago, IL 60611
1-800-621-8099 x. 2622

American Society of Addiction Medicine (ASAM)
12 West 21st Street
New York, NY 10010

Anesthetists in Recovery (AIR)
3413 Sailmaker Lane
Plano, TX 75023
24-hour hotline: 214-596-5382
  • Offers intervention services and treatment referrals.

Birds of a Feather
  • AA groups for airline pilots and, in some groups, other airline person-
    nel. Contact AA World Services for more information at 212-
    870-3400.

Employee Assistance Professional Association
2101 Wilson Blvd.
Arlington, VA 22201-3062
703-522-6272

Employee Assistance Society of North America (EASNA)
P.O. Box 3909
Oakpark, IL 60303
312-383-6668

Intercongregational Alcoholism Program (ICAP) Education
and Intervention, Inc.
1921 North Harlem Ave.
Chicago, IL 60635
312-637-1656
  • Educates Catholic nuns on alcoholism and
    refers nuns to treatment.

International Doctors in Alcoholics Anonymous (IDAA)
7250 France Ave. South, Suite 400C
Minneapolis, MN 55435
  • Annual AA meetings for both AA and Al-Anon members. Includes
    medical doctors, dentists, psychologists, veterinarians, and medical
    scientists.

International Lawyers in Alcoholics Anonymous (ILAA)
39 Smith Neck Road
Old Lyme, CT 06371
203-529-7474

International Nurses Anonymous (INA)
1020 Sunset Drive
Lawrence, KS 66044
913-842-3893
913-299-6838
• Support group for nurses in any twelve-step program.

International Pharmacists Anonymous (IPA)
c/o Nan D.
36 Cedar Grove Road
Annandale, NJ 08801
201-730-9072
201-735-2789

Impaired Nurse Network
c/o National Nurses Society on Addiction (NNSA)
2506 Gross Pointe Road
Evanston, IL 60201
312-475-1000
• Offers help with interventions and treatment referrals.

Narcotics Anonymous (NA)
P.O. Box 9999
Van Nuys, CA 91409
818-773-9999, phone
818-700-0700, fax

National Association for Children of Alcoholics (NACOA)
11426 Rockville Pike, #100
Rockville, MD 20852
301-468-0985

National Association of Native American
Children of Alcoholics (NANACOA)
P.O. Box 18736
Seattle, WA 98118
206-322-5601

National Clearinghouse for Alcohol and Drug Information (NCADI)
P.O. Box 2345
Rockville, MD 20847-2345
301-468-2600 or 1-800-729-6686

National Cocaine Hotline
1-800-COCAINE

National Council on Alcoholism and Drug Dependence, Inc.
(NCADD)
12 West 21st Street
New York, NY 10010
212-206-6770
1-800-NCA-CALL
Web site (www.ncadd.org)
- The NCADD operates the National Intervention Network (NIN) through many of its affiliates around the country. These affiliates provide certified interventionists to assist families and friends interested in organizing an intervention. The toll-free phone number is 1-800-654-4673. Interested persons can call this number in order to locate a certified interventionist in their area.

National Federation of Parents for a Drug-Free Youth
8730 Georgia Avenue, Suite 200
Silver Spring, MD 20910
1-800-554-5437

National Institute on Drug Abuse
Drug Abuse Information and Treatment Referral Hotline
1-800-662-HELP

New Life (Women for Sobriety)
P.O. Box 618
Quakertown, PA 18951
215-536-8026

Social Workers Helping Social Workers
South Street
Goshen, CT 06756
203-489-3808
- International network for MSWs offering support through meetings, newsletters, workshops, telephone contacts, and annual weekend conference/retreats.

Index

Action stage, 39-40
Active-oriented intervention model, 102-105
Acute detoxification, 34
Addiction
  and child abuse, 118-119
  diagnosis of, 30-31
  as a family illness, 66
  legal treatment of, 115-117
  as progressive illness, 55
  signs of, 28-30
  and social services, need for, 132-133
  stages of change with, 112
  treatment centers, 75
Addictive behavior, stages of change with, 112
Addictive disorder, 36
Addictive illness, 21
Administrative intervention, 80-81
  case study, 81
Adolescent intervention strategy, 87-89
  case examples, 96-100
Affirm (CARE), 6,137-138
Alcohol and drug screening, 135-136
Alcoholics Anonymous, 35,119
Alcoholism, defining, 26-28. *See also* Substance abuse
Ambivalence (and treatment), 39
American Medical Association, 74,78
American Society of Addiction Medicine, 35
American Society of Anesthesiology, 78
Americans with Disabilities Act, 56
Anglin, Doug, 119

Application form, 134-135
Argumentation (avoiding), 48

Behavior, employee change in, 84
Behaviors checklist, 58-60
Bissell, LeClair, 75
Blaming, 113

CAGE questionnaire, 26
Canavan, David I., 76
CARE, 5-6
  and intervention, 136-139
Change. *See* Intervention
Chemical dependency. *See also* Disease Model of Alcoholism and Drug Dependence
  education about, 112
  and social services, need for, 132-133
  as treatable disease, 22
Child abuse, and addiction, 118-119
Chronic illness, chemical dependence as, 8-9
Civil system changes, 118-119
Clinical examples of intervention, 106-111
  discussion of, 111-113
Collins, D. A., 37-38
Committee for impaired professionals, 18
Communicate (CARE), 5,137
Community resources, and treatment, 34
Conciliation board, 133
Concurrent illness, and intervention, 29

Order Your Own Copy of
This Important Book for Your Personal Library!

ADDICTION INTERVENTION
Strategies to Motivate Treatment-Seeking Behavior

_____ in hardbound at $29.95 (ISBN: 0-7890-0433-X)

_____ in softbound at $19.95 (ISBN: 0-7890-0434-8)

COST OF BOOKS_____	☐ **BILL ME LATER:** ($5 service charge will be added) (Bill-me option is good on US/Canada/Mexico orders only; not good to jobbers, wholesalers, or subscription agencies.)
OUTSIDE USA/CANADA/ MEXICO: ADD 20%_____	
POSTAGE & HANDLING_____ *(US: $3.00 for first book & $1.25 for each additional book)* *Outside US: $4.75 for first book & $1.75 for each additional book)*	☐ Check here if billing address is different from shipping address and attach purchase order and billing address information. Signature_____
SUBTOTAL_____	☐ **PAYMENT ENCLOSED: $**_____
IN CANADA: ADD 7% GST_____	☐ **PLEASE CHARGE TO MY CREDIT CARD.**
STATE TAX_____ *(NY, OH & MN residents, please add appropriate local sales tax)*	☐ Visa ☐ MasterCard ☐ AmEx ☐ Discover ☐ Diners Club Account #_____
FINAL TOTAL_____ *(If paying in Canadian funds, convert using the current exchange rate. UNESCO coupons welcome.)*	Exp. Date_____ Signature_____

Prices in US dollars and subject to change without notice.

NAME _____

INSTITUTION _____

ADDRESS _____

CITY _____

STATE/ZIP _____

COUNTRY _____ COUNTY (NY residents only) _____

TEL _____ FAX _____

E-MAIL_____

May we use your e-mail address for confirmations and other types of information? ☐ Yes   ☐ No

Order From Your Local Bookstore or Directly From
The Haworth Press, Inc.
10 Alice Street, Binghamton, New York 13904-1580 • USA
TELEPHONE: 1-800-HAWORTH (1-800-429-6784) / Outside US/Canada: (607) 722-5857
FAX: 1-800-895-0582 / Outside US/Canada: (607) 772-6362
E-mail: getinfo@haworth.com
PLEASE PHOTOCOPY THIS FORM FOR YOUR PERSONAL USE.

BOF96